Internet Skills for the Workplace

Empowering yourself for the digital age

GW00492873

Internet Handbooks

Books and Publishing on the Internet
Building a Web Site on the Internet
Careers Guidance on the Internet
Chat & Chat Rooms on the Internet
Creating a Home Page on the Internet
Discussion Forums on the Internet
Education & Training on the Internet
Exploring Yahoo! on the Internet
Finding a Job on the Internet
Free Software on the Internet
Free Stuff on the Internet
Getting Connected to the Internet
Getting Started on the Internet
Gardens & Gardening on the Internet
Graduate Job Hunting on the Internet
Homes & Property on the Internet
Human Resource Management on the Internet
Internet Explorer on the Internet
Internet for Schools
Internet for Students
Internet for Writers
Internet Skills for the Workplace
Law & Lawyers on the Internet
Managing the Internet in Your Organisation
Marketing Your Business on the Internet
Music & Musicians on the Internet
Naming a Web Site on the Internet
News and Magazines on the Internet
Overseas Job Hunting on the Internet
Personal Finance on the Internet
Promoting a Web Site on the Internet
Protecting Children on the Internet
Running a Shop on the Internet
Search Engines on the Internet
Shops & Shopping on the Internet
Studying English on the Internet
Studying Law on the Internet
Travel & Holidays on the Internet
Using Credit Cards on the Internet
Using Email on the Internet
Where to Find It on the Internet
Working from Home on the Internet
Your Privacy on the Internet

Other titles in preparation

Internet Skills
for the workplace

Empowering yourself for the digital age

Ian Hosker

BEd(Hons) MSc

www.internet-handbooks.co.uk

Other Internet Handbooks by Ian Hosker

Getting Connected to the Internet
Managing the Internet in Your Organisation

© Copyright 2002 by Ian Hosker.

First published in 2002 by Internet Handbooks Ltd, Plymbridge House, Estover Road, Plymouth PL6 7PY, United Kingdom.

Customer services tel:	(01752) 202301
Orders fax:	(01752) 202333
Customer services email:	cservs@plymbridge.com
Distributors web site:	www.plymbridge.com
Internet Handbooks web site:	www.internet-handbooks.co.uk

Note: The contents of this book are offered for the purposes of general guidance only and no liability can be accepted for any loss or expense incurred as a result of relying in particular circumstances on statements made in this book or by the web sites described. Readers are advised to check the current position with the appropriate authorities or professional advisers before entering into personal arrangements.

Case studies in this book are entirely fictional and any resemblance to real persons or organisations is entirely coincidental.

Typeset by PDQ Typesetting
Printed and bound by The Cromwell Press Ltd, Trowbridge, Wiltshire.

Contents

Contents

Before you begin

There is no great mystery to using the internet – honest!

There is a great deal of hype, misinformation and misunderstanding about what it is, what it can do, and the 'horrors' it holds in store for the innocent and the unwary. For those who have never experienced the internet, the picture can seem very confusing. The opportunities opened up by the internet are juxtaposed with the threats to children, bank accounts and computer systems – and perhaps the very fabric of society itself, if you take the darkest views at face value. As always, the reality is somewhere in between.

This book is about guiding you through the maze that is variously called the world wide web, internet or simply the net. There are essentially two places where people will interact with the internet: at home, or at work. While the principles are the same wherever you interact, this book introduces the basic the skills and usage in a workplace setting. Why? – simply because the ability to use the internet for business reference, and for communicating over large distances quickly and cheaply, is rightly seen as a very important new vocational skill. Electronic communication and information-gathering skills are now seen as essential for most non-manual occupations. This book is therefore structured as follows:

▶ Chapter 1 introduces the principles of the internet as a business research and communications tool. It then develops those relating to information gathering, and explains what, how and why?

▶ Chapter 2 introduces and helps you develop the basic skills in using the internet as an information-finding and collating tool, describing the structure of web site addresses ('URLs'), how to access web pages, and how to save and print them.

▶ Chapter 3 helps you develop the skills most associated with the frustrations newcomers experience with the internet – namely, efficient use of the web as a research and information-gathering tool. You will develop skills using basic and advanced search techniques.

▶ Chapter 4 describes and explains email, what it can do, particularly in a business setting, how it is structured and its relationship with the internet. Internet security issues are also discussed in this chapter, although there are frequent references to this issue throughout the book.

▶ Chapter 5 then helps you develop the skills in creating and sending email messages, including how to use the email system to transfer documents to any number of recipients.

▶ Chapter 6 looks at the other side of the coin: receiving and responding to email messages, including how to scan documents sent to you for the presence of viruses. It also describes what you should do if you do find a virus!

▶ Finally, chapter 7 ties it all together. You are given a series of scenarios for you to test your developing skills and experience. Each scenario is a realistic simulation of the workplace in which electronic communications via the internet is a requirement.

Since this is a book to learn from, each chapter (except chapter 7) begins with a set of learning outcomes, and ends with a checklist of those outcomes. Use the checklists to monitor your skill and knowledge development.

Finally, we should mention the software applications used in the skills development chapters. The two most common applications for use with the internet are Microsoft and Netscape. Between them, they account for the vast majority of internet users. The versions described in this book are the ones current at the time of writing – Internet Explorer and Outlook Express version 5, Outlook 2000, and Netscape 6. The skills development chapters (2, 3, 5, and 6) are divided into sections devoted to each of these applications.

You will notice that some illustrations in the book have small areas that appear to be smudged and blurred. This is because they have been created from screen shots of real email or account settings, and so confidential information has been rendered unreadable.

If you have never used the internet before, prepare to be amazed – and only occasionally frustrated! If you have any comments about the book or your experiences on the internet, feel free to email me at the address shown below.

Ian Hosker
ianhosker@internet-handbooks.co.uk

1 The internet at work

In this chapter, we will explore:

▶ *learning outcomes for this chapter*
▶ *Why are internet skills important?*
▶ *Can I ignore the internet?*
▶ *One person – multiple tasks!*
▶ *Cost-effective communications – email*
▶ *Researching business information and the internet*
▶ *Your learning outcomes checklist*

Learning outcomes for this chapter

The aim of this chapter is to examine the way in which developing internet skills can benefit you, your career development, and the organisation you work for. By the end of the chapter you should:

1. Know why internet skills matter in the workplace.

2. Understand the risks of ignoring the benefits of the internet in the workplace.

3. Understand the value of the internet for fast, cost-effective communications.

4. Understand issues of managing workload, information and communication flow.

5. Understand the value of the internet as a business information research tool.

Why are internet skills important?

Within a very short space of time there has been an explosive growth in the use of the internet by businesses. Interestingly, there has been a similar growth in the development of mobile communications technology, and the two are linked. Technology companies are busy right now developing equipment and software which integrates mobile communications systems to the internet. No matter where you are, if you have the right mobile technology you can access the internet and its vast information and communications capabilities.

The pace of change is exceptionally rapid. This has resulted in companies and their employees reviewing the way they work. The impact of this development must be something like that experienced during the industrial revolution in the late eighteenth and nineteenth centuries. Now, as then, the explosive pace of change was not immediate. A psychological shift is needed, where new technology is accepted and embraced. Only then is a market created for it, and a momentum built up.

And what has been the effect on vocational skill requirements? C&IT (communications and information technology) skills are in more demand now than ever before. Even the name of the skills has changed over the space of a few years: information technology (IT) to information and communications technology (ICT), and now C&IT.

This change reflects the shift in emphasis of the technology. A generation ago, computers were machines that relatively few people had access to – they were programmers or data entry clerks. Computers were generally used for business records, and there may have been one or two computers in the office. They were also incredibly expensive – and midgets in terms of today's computing power. Now, of course, every employee can have his or her own computer, each with a computing power beyond the imagination of those early users.

The new skills and knowledge required
As a result of these changes, employers require three types of skills and knowledge to make effective use of their technology-based systems. They are:

1. Technical knowledge and skills to install and maintain computer systems and programs.

2. C&IT cultural awareness. Employers have a developed sense of what technology is able to do, and how it can be applied to specific business tasks and functions.

3. Operational skills, where employees have a high level of competence in using specific programs for specific tasks and job roles.

This book is about skills and knowledge associated with the last two groups in the list. Employers are listing internet-based skills as being desirable or essential in an increasing number of job specifications, and not only for relatively senior posts. The skills are seen as being required across the whole range of administrative, supervisory and managerial functions.

Can I ignore the internet?

You can ignore the internet, just as you can ignore any opportunity, but you may have to pay a price for doing so. Of course, we have to recognise some unpleasant and controversial aspects of internet use, and the workplace has not been immune from those.

▶ *Example* – There has been concern about the ethical and legal aspects of employers monitoring their employees' use of the internet. Is it right for employees to use company time to send private emails, or to surf the web for private research and information-gathering purposes?

Many companies have developed, or are in the process of developing, policies on the private use of the internet by employees.

The technology has created an opportunity for information gathering and dissemination at a speed and volume, and over vast distances (including extra-terrestrial space) that is almost unimaginable. This makes it difficult to control except by those individuals who are participating. In other words, it is users – not nations or governments – that are developing the internet. The internet generates business opportunities, and responds to them, at the same time.

On the day-to-day level of business operation, as the cost of technology falls, public confidence and interest in the internet rises. As the number and range of people hooked up to the internet also increases, even the smallest of businesses will have no option but to respond to this. And the cost does not need to be high.

The economic arguments
There are very strong economic arguments for making greater use of the internet:

1. To gather business information about competitors and new market opportunities, from government agencies regarding regulations and support for business initiatives, or simply to book travel and accommodation for business trips and conferences.

2. To maintain regular contact with customers and colleagues. Organisations can exchange information and documents half way across the world more or less instantaneously. Video-conferencing may negate the need for many people to use expensive air travel and hotel services.

Of course, there is no legal or moral argument that we must all become part of the internet, either as companies or as individuals. The pressure to take part is placed on organisations by their customers and competitors who have already embraced the technology and culture. There is much debate about the effect this is having on the labour market, where the emphasis is on a 'knowledge-based' economy.

▶ The aim of this book is not to debate the pros, cons or legitimacy of the internet revolution, but simply to help you develop the skills. Without these skills, which can also benefit people and families outside the workplace, people may even find themselves excluded from some areas of future employment.

One person: multiple tasks!

The internet enables you to integrate several tasks at the same time.

▶ *Example* – You can receive and reply to email messages while still word processing a report. If you need to write a report and find that a piece of useful information is missing, it is an easy task to email a colleague for the information while you are still working on the report itself, or use the internet to search for the information from relevant web sites.

Our ability to do this results from the capability of modern computers to 'multi-task'. In other words, they have sufficient power and speed to allow more than one computer program to be used at any one time. Thus, you can have your word processor (one program) active while you open the web browser (another program) to search for information from web sites. You can even copy sections of a web page text or images, or even copy whole pages and 'paste' them into your report! (subject of course to copyright law).

Coping with the pressure of change
It has been argued that computers and the internet (email, in particular) play a major role in a massive increase in work related stress, and consequential illnesses. It is difficult to verify or quantify such arguments, but it is probably true that the sheer capability of technology to process and transfer information between individuals is unprecedented in history, and this requires people to work rather differently than was formerly the case. For example, you will need to be:

(a) Better at self-management, particularly in terms of time management.

(b) Better able to identify information that is important and so needs to be remembered, and find ways of storing all other information in a way that can be recalled should it be needed. You also need to be able to identify information that will not be needed and so can be ditched safely!

(c) Better at prioritising responses to electronic communications sent to you. Some of this will be requests for information, instructions from managers, tempting offers from manufacturers or suppliers, or the product of the office 'spammer' (the person who emails the latest joke or other nonsense to everyone in the company).

(d) More considerate of colleagues. The ease of electronic communications makes it so effortless to contact people on the spur of the moment – or even at the last moment – with unreasonable requests to respond within the hour!

Expectations and reality
The problem lies not with computers or the internet, but with people. Our expectations can often be unrealistically high because the technology lulls us into a sense that outcomes can be achieved as easily as the process of requesting them!

For example, I ordered a mobile phone via the internet on a Tuesday morning; it was delivered on Wednesday morning, less than 24 hours later. This can raise expectations about future deliveries and breed dissatisfaction with slower response times that are actually still quite reasonable.

Cost-effective communications: email

Electronic communication is cheap when compared with the cost of paper-based systems. It is also quick and can be almost immediate. You can send simple messages with ease. You can even attach documents and files to your message so they are received at the other end within seconds or minutes of sending them.

This cost-effectiveness is further enhanced by the ability to send the same email to as many recipients as you like, wherever they may be. You only have to send it once. Your internet service provider (ISP) will distribute copies to each recipient you have listed. The value of this to business is enormous:

1. The speed of communication means that important information and documents can be shared and responded to very quickly.

2. Geography is no barrier. The recipients might be in the next office or half way around the world, or both, if more than one recipient is involved.

Suppliers and customers do not necessarily need to be located near to each other. A graphic designer in Penzance can communicate with and supply a client in central London (or Brussels!) as easily as if they were in the same town.

We could say that electronic communication is also more environmentally friendly. That can be a difficult one to argue, because the promise of the paperless office never quite materialised. But, in other ways, the vision has materialised. We no longer always have to hold face-to-face meetings with colleagues. Some business discussions can take place via email or through video-conferencing.

Email and video-conferencing
For most people, standard email communication has become the norm. Apart from the visual aspect of video-conferencing, the main difference between the two methods of communication is time.

▶ Video-conferencing occurs in so-called 'real time'. This means that it is live.

▶ Email may be fast, but receiving it is not necessarily immediate.

▶ Video-conferencing requires all parties to be connected to the internet at the same time. Email does not.

▶ Email messages, once sent, will remain stored by the recipients'

ISPs computers until such time as they connect and request stored email.

Email communication methods are described in chapters 4 to 6.

Researching business information and the internet

One of the main complaints about the internet is the difficulty of getting the information you want from it. The perception is that it is poorly organised, even chaotic. Users are unable to search systematically to gain information they want. A user will try to seek information in a rational way, but end up with irrelevant responses from the internet.

What is often just as depressing is that a search for information (see chapter 3) may literally turn up millions of references. This is far too many to trawl through for the gem of information you need. To use the internet effectively calls for a systematic approach. You need a plan, and this will be discussed in more detail in chapter 3.

This perception arises out of unrealistic expectations of the internet. It is a truly vast system of information pages and databases, with over a thousand million web pages available. It therefore requires some skill to ask the right questions and sift the rubbish from the useful, and then to sift the most valuable information from the less useful.

The problem is in the way in which the internet has been promoted, and continues to be promoted. This creates the expectation that you just can sit in front of the computer's monitor, type in a request, and receive an intelligent and perfectly formed response. It doesn't quite work like that!

I once heard a computer salesman's pitch to a bemused and somewhat reticent customer which went something like this:

'The internet is amazing. There's absolutely nothing you can't find on the internet. There's information on everything'.

The salesman went on to demonstrate the accuracy of this confident assertion and searched on some subject or other. The response was: no information found! It is not a perfect or simple system, but it is a powerful and informative business tool, providing you know how to use it effectively.

Organisations need information so they can operate efficiently. A major problem they face is that of knowing what information is available and how to obtain it. The ability to find and make sense of information on the internet is a valuable asset in the workplace. There are ways of gathering and presenting information from the internet which make it useful or persuasive. Chapters 2 and 3 are all about how to do this, and they look at how you can be systematic in your approach, thereby saving time.

▶ The tutorials at the end of the chapters will test your knowledge and skills with exercises on information gathering and presentation.

The medium and the message
People are getting mixed messages about the value of the internet. There seem be two camps: those whose praise of the system of information transfer knows no bounds, and those whose criticism equally knows no bounds. There is also a third camp: those who have no experience of the internet, and so are confused by the mixed messages sent out by the other two camps.

Part of the problem rests with internet companies, especially the internet service providers (ISPs), who market the system as if it were soap powder. Nor is it helped by enthusiastic internet users who insist that this is the only way to go, and the two-thirds of the UK population not hooked up are luddites! (machine-smashers of the early industrial revolution).

The reality of the internet is that it is neither magical nor a panacea. It can be frustrating when you cannot find the information you need through a search engine (this will be considered in chapter 3). If you search the internet for information on *hotels*, the number of entries returned will be overpowering! After all, internet search engines are probably the largest databases in the world and, as with all databases, you need to be as specific as possible to make sure sites that are a close match become listed in the search results pages.

It is not, as many ISPs would have us believe, a system that you can simply pick up and use. There are some basic principles and 'rules' which need to be learned before it becomes an enjoyable, let alone an effective, business tool. So, let chapters 2 and 3 introduce you to the skills and techniques which will make using the internet as a research tool as fruitful and enjoyable an experience for you as possible.

Your learning outcomes checklist

At the beginning of the chapter you were given a list of things you should know or be able to do by the time you had worked through the chapter. These learning outcomes are listed again for you to consider. Use the checklist overleaf as a self-assessment tool to see if you can confidently say you have achieved them. Where you feel that you have not achieved a learning outcome, or would like to have another go to make sure, a pointer suggests the section to revisit.

The internet at work..

Outcome	Achieved	If not, or want to recap, revisit
Know why internet skills are important in the workplace.		Why are internet skills important? Can I ignore it?
Understand the possible consequences of ignoring the benefits of the internet in the workplace.		Can I ignore it?
Understand the value of the internet for fast, cost-effective communications.		Cost-effective communications: email.
Understand the issues associated with managing workload, information and communication flow.		One person: multiple tasks!
Understand the value of the internet as a business information research tool.		Can I ignore it? Researching business information and the internet.

2 Visiting web sites

In this chapter, we will explore:

▶ *learning outcomes for this chapter*
▶ *what is a web site address?*
▶ *what are the features of a web browser?*
▶ *how do I start my web browser program?*
▶ *how can I view an organisation's web site?*
▶ *what are links and hyperlinks?*
▶ *how to revisit web sites*
▶ *using your browser's History function*
▶ *creating bookmarks*
▶ *using a bookmark to visit a site*
▶ *deleting bookmarks*
▶ *can I keep the information once I have found it?*
▶ *tutorial*
▶ *your learning outcomes checklist*

. . . .

Learning outcomes for this chapter

This chapter is concerned with using the internet as a tool for gathering business information. By the end of this chapter you will:

1. Understand why effective searching of the internet is of value in business.

2. Know how a web site address is structured.

3. Know what a web browser does.

4. Understand the purpose of each of your browser's features.

5. Be able to use the web browser to visit a web site using its address.

6. Be able to re-visit sites using the 'history' facility.

7. Be able to use 'bookmarks'.

8. Know how to save web pages to view 'offline' and to print them.

What is a web site address?

Technically, a web site address is called its **uniform resource locator** (URL); you will come across this term frequently on the internet. The URL is a way of uniquely identifying a web site, or individual pages within the site. The following examples are imaginary URLs that show their general structure:

http://www.somewebsite.com

http://www.somewebsite.com/subweb

http://www.somewebsite.com/page.htm

https://www.somewebsite.com/page.htm

These need to be explained, and then some more information provided about variations you will come across.

http://www.somewebsite.com
The http:// part of a URL tends to be ignored these days. Its role is to simply tell the computer that it is being required to look up a web site. It is being included here because it still exists and will be described for the sake of completeness. When you come to look at how to call up a web site on your computer, the URL used will omit http://

This is how the URL breaks down into its constituent components:

1. *http://* This is shorthand for **hypertext transfer protocol**. The core programming language for pages displayed by a web browser is called hypertext mark-up language (HTML). Thus, http:// tells the computer that what follows is an internet site (or a particular page within the site).

2. *www.somewebsite.com* This is referred to as the **domain name**. Each domain name is unique to a particular web site. The 'www' instructs the computer that it is dealing with the world wide web. The full stops (or 'dots' as they are called) are important because they separate the various components of the URL. Don't omit them, or your computer will be unable to locate the address.

All domain names have a suffix giving additional information about the web site, such as country of registration or type of organisation. For example, a web site could be '.co.uk' or '.com'. Table 2.1 shows some of the possible domain name combinations based on 'somewebsite'. Note: each one is a legitimate domain name in its own right and so could be used to name separate web sites.

The list of nine domain name combinations in Table 2.1 is not exhaustive. It simply illustrates the potential, and real, confusion that has arisen from the massive growth in internet use. Once the preserve of American academic institutions and government agencies, the internet is now accessible to anyone with a half-decent computer, modem and phone line.

Possible domain name	What it means
www.somewebsite.com	The so-called 'dot com' is American in origin and is used by commercial and industrial organisations.
www.somewebsite.org	American in origin, non-commercial organisations tend to use this to show their charitable or non-commercial status.
www.somewebsite.gov	Probably an American government agency.
www.somewebsite.co.uk	A domain name normally associated with a commercial or industrial organisation in the UK.
www.somewebsite.sch.uk	This would be the web site of a UK-based school.
www.somewebsite.ac.uk	A UK university or further education college.
www.somewebsite.org.uk	A UK-based charity or non-commercial organisation.
www.somewebsite.gov.uk	A UK government department or agency web site.
www.somewebsite.net	An organisation not aligning itself to any of the other formats that may lead you to assume the nature of the site. This tends to be more 'global' in flavour and implies belonging to a broad network of interests.

Table 2.1: Possible domain names based on 'somewebsite'

New top level domains

The internet is awash with registered web sites owned by a huge diversity of individuals and organisations. As a result, the 'old' suffixes do not really apply any more.

At the time of writing, seven new 'top-level domains' have been agreed by ICANN (Internet Corporation for Assigned Names and Number), the body responsible for regulating domain names. These will reflect the diversity of individuals and organisations participating in the internet. Table 2.2 lists the additional domain name extensions being introduced.

Domain name extension	For whom it is intended
.pro	For use by professionals – e.g. lawyers, accountants, doctors.
.name	For use by an individual – Aunt Agatha's web site!
.biz	For use by any business.
.info	Restrictions have not been placed on the use of this suffix, but it is likely to appeal to providers of information services.
.aero	Air transport and aerospace industry.
.museum	As implied by the name, museums will use this suffix.
.coop	For use by non-profit making co-operatives.

Table 2.2. The new additional domain name extensions.

Visiting web sites ....

www.somewebsite.com/subweb

A web site may sometimes be very large and complex. If so, it may be broken down into more manageable areas, or subwebs, each devoted to a particular aspect of the site's content. In effect, they are mini web sites. By specifying the particular subweb within the URL like this, you can gain quick access to that part of the web site without having to go through the main 'gateway'. The first part of the URL is followed by a slash (/) and then the name of the subweb.

You may already be familiar with the principles of file management on a computer – where files of a similar type are organised together in electronic 'folders' – or a paper-based system of filing cabinets in an office. Web site organisation is very similar. Figure 2.1 illustrates the system.

Figure 2.1. A web site may be organised into a series of sub-webs, each with its own set of web pages.

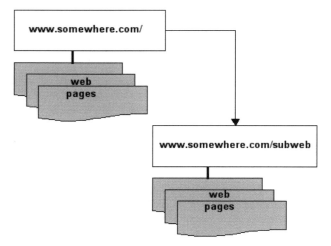

It can get more complicated because a subweb may in turn have its own subwebs. Thus, a URL could look like this (and even longer):

www.somewebsite.com/subweb/subweb2/

However, good web designers are aware of the complications for users and work hard to create sites that are easy for people to find their way around.

www.somewebsite.com/page.htm

A web site is made up of any number of individual electronic pages of information called **web pages**. If someone wants to point you directly to information easily, the best way is to give you the URL of the appropriate page on a web site. The first part of the URL is already familiar. It is then followed by the slash (/) symbol and the name of the page.

▶ A web page is an electronic file in its own right, much like a spreadsheet or word-processed document. As such, web pages have to be stored in a particular electronic format that can be read by the system that has to use it.

A file name has two parts: a name and a file extension (the three-letter suffix that follows a full stop). For example, this chapter was written in Word 2000 and was named: ch02.doc. The '.doc' extension tells the computer that it is a Word document. Web pages are no different. The language used to write most pages is HTML, as was explained earlier. These pages have the extension '.htm' or '.html'. (There are several other possible extensions to the page name such as '.asp', but we won't worry about them now as they relate to more complex sites that operate as interactive databases.)

So the URL given at the top of this section is the exact location on the internet of a specific web page within a given web site. If the page happens to be within a sub-web, then the URL will simply reflect that, for example:

www.somewebsite.com/subweb/page.htm

https:// (secure servers)
If the URL begins with the prefix https:// you know that you are visiting a secure server (a **server** is a computer which stores and makes available internet or network material). This means that the site is the subject of a very high degree of protection. Information sent to and from the server is encrypted so that if intercepted it cannot be read. In theory, the site is also safe from 'hacking', a deliberate attempt to access the confidential information stored on the server.

Secure servers are used wherever confidential information is stored, and to which only limited access is allowed. For example, online shopping requires the buyer to provide details of credit or debit cards while online as part of the purchasing process. Clearly this is a security issue for the buyer. A secure server is therefore used to collect and store that information. Similarly, online banking requires the use of secure servers.

What are the features of a web browser?

To gain access to a web site or a specific page within the site, you need a program that will act as the interface between your computer and the internet. This is called the **web browser** and will display web pages on your computer's monitor.

The two giants in this field are Microsoft's Internet Explorer, and Netscape. In this book, the current versions of both programs will be described (i.e. Internet Explorer 5.5 and Netscape 6). There are other browsers – quite a few in fact – but these two dominate the market and have been rivals for quite a number of years. It seems strange now, but in the mid 1990s these programs had a retail selling price, but the battle for dominance ended that. If not already installed on your machine, they can be found free on computer magazine give-away cover disks! More often than not, they will come through the post as a part of a promotion to get you sign up to an internet service provider.

A common browser interface
There are universal features of all web browsers. This means they look and handle in very similar ways. Figures 2.2 and 2.3 show the browser windows of Internet Explorer and Netscape Navigator.

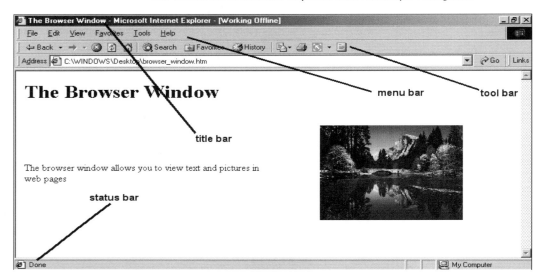

Figure 2.2. Microsoft's Internet Explorer browser window.

Figure 2.3. Netscape's browser window.

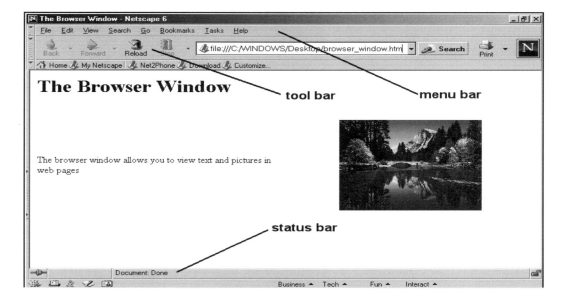

General browser features

1. *Title bar* – This is positioned at the top of the window. This space shows the title of the displayed page.

2. *Menu bar* – Each of the words on this bar produce drop-down menus when you click on them. These menus provide access to a range of actions. If you are familiar with word processing or other windows based programs, then you will be familiar with these menus. You will look at some of these functions later in the chapter.

3. *Tool bar* – These small icons provide shortcuts to the more commonly used actions. Table 2.3 shows what each of the main icons does.

Table 2.3. Tool bar icons.

Internet Explorer	Netscape	What it does
⇐ Back ▾ ⇒ ▾	Back Forward	Moves the viewer sequentially between pages previously visited during this Internet session.
⊗	Stop	The Stop button allows you to stop a page loading – a sort of emergency stop that is useful if you made a mistake or the page is taking too long to load and you decide to move on.
⟳	Reload	The refresh or reload button tells the browser to reload the current page. Useful when a page fails to load properly.
⌂	Home	Return to Start Page button. Use this if you want to return to your browser's start page.
Search	Search	The search button opens the browser's default search engine. This topic is covered in the next chapter.
Favorites		Opens the list of bookmarked web pages for you to revisit in Explorer. Bookmarks are accessed via the Bookmarks menu in Netscape.
History		In Explorer this button opens a side panel showing your browsing history. Netscape uses a different method (see later in this chapter).
🖨	Print	This prints the page you are viewing.
✉▾		Opens your email program in Explorer.

Display window
The web page is displayed in this space.

Visiting web sites ....

Status bar
This bar keeps you informed of what is happening as you instruct the browser to find a web page. For example, it will indicate that it is looking for the site, located the site, is downloading the page, and then is 'Done' once the page is loaded.

How do I start my web browser program?

Method 1
(a) Click the **Start** button to open the start menu (figure 2.4). Select **Programs** from the menu.

Figure 2.4. Starting up your web browser from the Start menu on the task bar.

(b) Select the web browser program from the Programs menu. Figure 2.4 shows Netscape being selected.

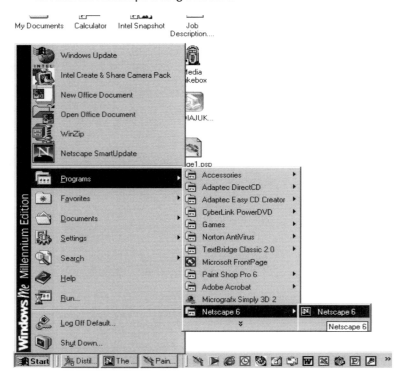

The browser program will start. However, what happens next depends on the way your computer has been set up. The browser will search for what is called the **start page**, the web site it has been set to open when the program starts. However, to do this the computer needs to be connected to the internet.

At a place of study, or in the workplace, a machine may be part of a group of computers all linked together on a network. If so, the network probably has a permanent link to the internet via a special computer (server) that controls the network. In this case, when you start the browser, the internet link will be made automatically.

If your computer is not on a network, or if you are using a compu-ter at home, access to the internet will be by a 'dial-up connection' to your **internet service provider** (ISP). Figure 2.5 shows the dial-up connection dialog box for Internet Explorer in Windows ME. It looks similar in Windows 98 or Windows 95. The user name assigned to you by your ISP will be displayed, but you will need to type in your password. Next, click the Connect button. The computer then dials your ISP's computer via the computer's modem and your phone line. Once connected to your ISP, the start page will be loaded and displayed in your browser window.

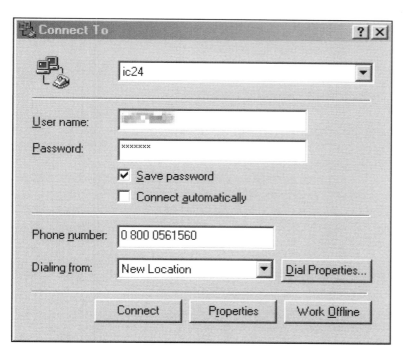

Figure 2.5. The Dial-up connection box. You will need your user name and password to access your ISP's services.

Method 2

There are usually two shortcuts to starting your web browser that eliminate the need to access the program through the Start menu.

Figure 2.6 shows part of the Task Bar at the bottom of the monitor screen. This is visible at all times and allows you to access your web browser and email programs. Depending on how your computer is set up, you may also be able to start other programs from here as well. To open your web browser, click once on the browser icon. The browser starts automatically and looks for the start page.

Figure 2.6. You may have a short cut to your web browser on your task bar.

Visiting web sites ....

Figure 2.7. Shortcuts to
your browser may also
be found on your
Desktop monitor screen.

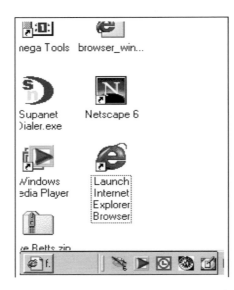

Figure 2.7 shows a part of the desktop window that your computer displays when it is not running any programs. The desktop enables you to access a range of programs and services quickly. This includes your web browser and email programs. Small pictures (icons) represent programs. To open a program, double-click on the icon. In figure 2.7, you can see the icons for Internet Explorer and Netscape. You don't need to have both programs installed on your computer. Most people, or the organisations they work for, have a favourite web browser and tend to stick with it. Internet Explorer is the most widely used.

How can I view an organisation's web site?

In an ideal world you will know the URL of every web site you are likely to visit. If you do know the URL, this section explains how to access the site. Earlier in the chapter, the structure of a URL was described, and it is sometimes worth attempting an informed guess. Most organisations try to register a URL that reflects their names. Try variations on the theme of the name.

Example
If a company is called Acme Fireworks, try writing down a few variations of the possible URLs. This list gives an idea of what they might be:

> www.acme.co.uk
> www.acmefireworks.co.uk
> www.acme.com
> www.acmefireworks.com
> www.acme-fireworks.co.uk
> www.acme-fireworks.com

You can work through this list using the techniques described in this section. Of course, none of these may be correct. In that case, you will need to use a search engine to find the site you want – but more of that in the next chapter.

If you do know the URL of the site or web page you want to visit, there are two ways of getting there.

Method 1 – Web browser already open
If you already have your web browser open then follow this method. When you type in the URL of your chosen web site, or specific web page, you can omit the 'http://'. The browser will automatically interpret 'www' as a request for a web site.

Internet Explorer
(a) Position your mouse pointer anywhere within the **address bar** near the top. Click the left-hand mouse button once. This will highlight any text in the bar.

(b) Type the URL of the web site you want to visit. This will automatically replace the text in the box with what you are typing (see figure 2.8).

Figure 2.8. Internet Internet Explorer. To view a web page, type the URL in the Address box, then press the Enter key on your keyboard.

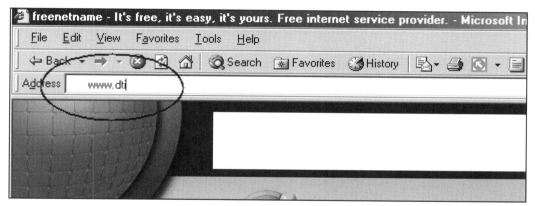

(c) Press the Enter key on the keyboard. The browser will now search for the site you have requested. You will see how this is progressing in the bottom left-hand side of the status bar. This indicates that the browser is contacting, and then connecting with, the site. When the page has finally been loaded into the browser, the message in the status bar reads: Done.

Netscape
1. Position your mouse pointer in the address bar (Netscape calls it the **location bar**). Then double-click the left-hand mouse button to highlight the text already there.

2. Type the URL of the web site. This will automatically replace the text (see figure 2.9).

Figure 2.9. Netscape. Type the URL in the Location bar, then press the Enter key on your keyboard.

3. Press the Enter key on the keyboard to start loading the web page. Progress in loading the page can be observed at the bottom left-hand side of the status bar, as with Internet Explorer. When the page is completely loaded into the browser, the message will read: Document done.

Method 2 – Web browser not open
If you want to access the internet, it is often to visit a particular site. You can save a little time by using this shortcut method of accessing a particular page. If you then want to visit other sites, you can simply adopt method 1 above to continue your internet session.

1. Point your mouse arrow at the Start button on the task bar. Then click the left-hand mouse button to activate the Start menu. Select Run from the menu, to open the run dialog box (see figure 2.10)

2. Type the URL of the web site in the run dialog box. Then click the *OK* button (see figure 2.10).

Figure 2.10. Typing the URL in the Run dialog box is a slightly quicker way of getting to the web site.

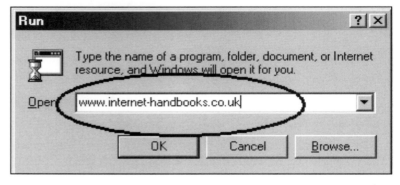

3. The computer's default browser will open and try to access the web site. If your computer is part of a company network it will probably automatically access the internet. If not, it will open the dial-up dialog box as descried earlier in the chapter. You will then need to enter your user name and password before clicking the Connect button (see the section on **How do I start my web browser program?**)

What are links and hyperlinks?

Earlier in the chapter, we described a web site as a series of electronic pages of information. When you type in the URL of a web site without specifying a particular page, the browser will open the introductory page of that site – usually referred to as the **home page**. Its name is usually:

index.htm

or

index.html

You don't need to include the page name as you type in the URL into the address bar. The browser will assume that you mean the home page. This page is important because its function is to provide a way of accessing other parts of the web site. It is a sort of contents page.

Once you have arrived at a web site, you will want to visit other pages within the site (a process called **navigation**). To do this, you need to look out for **hyperlinks**, areas on the page that are linked to another part of the web site. When the mouse arrow moves onto a hyperlink it changes to a small pointing hand (see figure 2.11). This shows that it is a link (hyperlink). The web site or web page to which the hyperlink is linked will appear in the task bar.

Figure 2.11.The mouse pointer changes to a pointing hand when it is over a hyperlink.

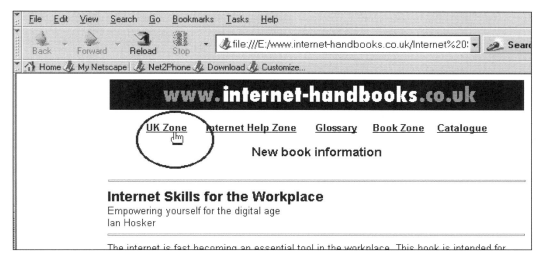

▶ *Links* – Any object on the page could be a hyperlink – for example text, image, or part of an image. The object will have text to say what area of the site it is linked to. Clicking once on the link with the left-hand mouse button will take you to the linked area or page.

Types of hyperlinks

▶ *Internal and external links* – Most links tend to be to other pages in the same web site or, if a page is very long, to another part of the page you are currently viewing. These are internal links. However, some links will take the visitor to another web site altogether, and these are called external links.

▶ *Email links* – Many web sites encourage you to contact an individual or organisation by email. To make this easy for you, the web designer puts a special email link on the page. If you click it, it will activate your email program ready-addressed to the recipient (see figure 2.12). The message in the task bar of your browser will look something like this:

mailto:jo@thisisp.co.uk

The 'mailto:' part of the message indicates that it is an email link. The second part is the recipient's email address. All you have to do is type your message and send it. Of course, this assumes you have an email account either with your ISP or in your organisation's computer network.

Figure 2.12. An email link will be denoted by the 'mailto:' caption on the browser's task bar. The type of hyperlink will always be shown on the task bar.

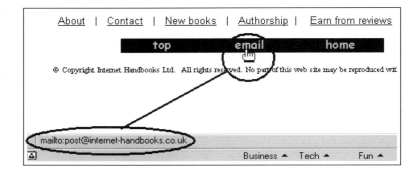

► *FTP links* – Clicking on a link of this type will activate a process that will transfer a file to your computer. The process is called **downloading**. It involves a technology called **file transfer protocol** (FTP). This is frequently used by web sites that offer the facility to download computer programs and upgrades (e.g. Microsoft), or useful documents. The message in the taskbar of the browser will look something like this:

ftp://ftp.thisisp.com/downloads

The 'ftp://' part of the message tells you that the link is to an FTP server. The rest of the message refers to the location of the file to be transferred.

► *Anchor (bookmark on a page)* – In very long pages, it is often useful to create anchors on the page. Anchors are bookmarks at specific parts of the page. A hyperlink can then be created on another part of the page so that when it is clicked, the reader will be taken directly to the anchor. A good example of this is where a page has a table of contents at the top. Each line is a hyperlink to a particular anchor. Each anchor must have a name to distinguish it from any other anchors on the page. The message in the task bar will look something like this:

http://www.thisisp.co.uk/page.htm#anchor

The anchor is denoted by the 'page.htm#anchor' part of the message. The hash mark # shows that the link is to an anchor on the page and that 'anchor' will be the anchor name (e.g. top, bottom, 1, contents, etc).

How to revisit web sites

Is there an easy way to revisit sites?
You may often want to return to particular web sites. The reason could be that:

1. The sites are rich sources of information or services, such as the web sites of potential suppliers or customers.

2. The volume of information on the site may be too much to explore at any one time.

3. You may wish to return to check your own information about an organisation.

There are several ways of ensuring an easy return to a previously visited site. Of course, you could memorise or make a note of the URL, but you could easily lose that information. Web browsers have built into them several functions that allow revisits 'without tears'. Which of these you use will depend on circumstances as well as personal reference. In practice, there are two situations where you will want to revisit: during the course of a current internet session or at some point during later internet sessions.

Revisiting during a current internet session
During any single internet session, you may visit dozens of web sites and pages as you click your way through links that interest you. As you do so, the browser remembers where you have been and in what order you viewed the pages. Figure 2.13 shows the **Back** and **Forward** buttons in Internet Explorer and Netscape.

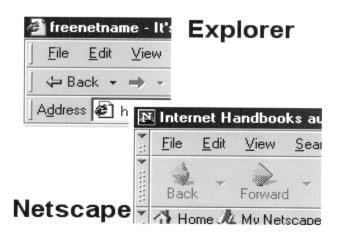

Figure 2.13. The Forward and Back buttons enable you to view pages that you have already visited during your current browsing session.

Visiting web sites ....

Clicking the Back button will take you back sequentially through the pages you have viewed. If you keep clicking, you will eventually end up at the first page you viewed. Clicking the Forward button can only be used after using the Back button as it takes you forward sequentially, ending up at the last page you viewed. It's rather like flicking backwards and forwards through a book to review pages you have already read.

This facility is useful for two reasons:

1. It allows you to revisit a page very quickly.

2. It is easy to get 'lost' during an internet session. You can become carried away by following interesting links, and then forget where you started from. The Back arrow is a useful way of retracing your steps.

Revisiting during a later internet session
There are two methods to help you revisit web sites.

▶ *History* – your computer keeps a record (History) of your browsing activity for around three weeks. After this time, it ditches the record to conserve memory.

▶ *Bookmarking/Favorites* – you can bookmark a site as you view it. This keeps a permanent record of the site's URL in memory. When you want to return to the site, you select the bookmark and the browser automatically seeks the web page. This record is called a Bookmark in Netscape and a Favorite (correct spelling) in Internet Explorer.

Using your browser's History function

Browsers also record your browsing history, and record the pages you have viewed. Your computer will also be set to keep copies of all pages visited for a fixed period of time. In Internet Explorer the default setting is 20 days. After this time, the record is deleted from the computer's memory to conserve memory.

Internet Explorer

1. Click the History button on the tool bar (circled in figure 2.14). This will open a sidebar as shown in figure 2.14. Note that this contains several 'folders' that contain the information on the sites you have visited during the previous three weeks.

2. If you know roughly when you visited the site, click on the folder in the sidebar to view the sites visited that day or week (figure 2.15).

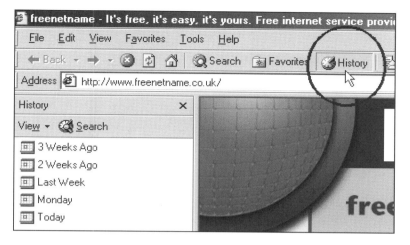

Figure 2.14. Internet Explorer. The History button provides a shortcut method of accessing sites you have visited in the previous few weeks.

Figure 2.15. Internet Explorer. Click on the folder to open shortcuts to sites visited that week or day.

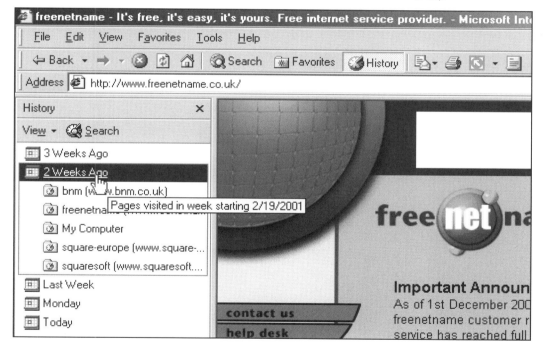

3. Click on the folder of the web site you want to revisit. This will open a list of the pages visited (figure 2.16).

4. Select the page you want to visit and click on it. The browser will call up and display the page (figure 2.17).

Visiting web sites ....

Figure 2.16. Internet
Explorer. Click on the
site's folder to view
shortcuts to the pages
visited.

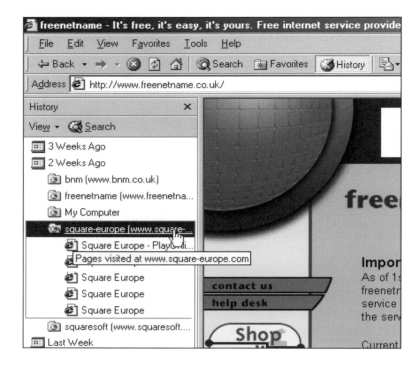

Figure 2.17. Internet
Explorer. Click on the
page shortcut to reload
the page into your
browser.

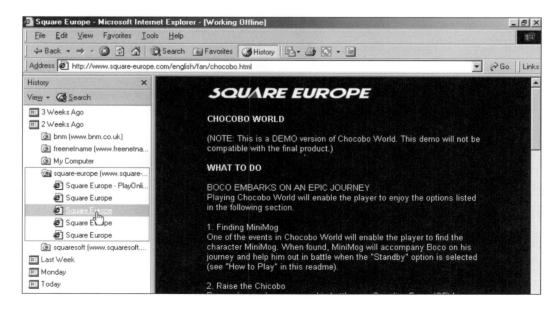

Netscape Navigator
Select the **Tasks** menu on the menu bar, and select **Tools** > **History** from the menu (figure 2.18). You will now see a box open with a list of web pages visited (figure 2.19). Point to the page you want to revisit and double-click the left mouse button. The browser will revisit the site and download the page.

Figure 2.18. In Netscape, you access your browsing history via the Tasks menu.

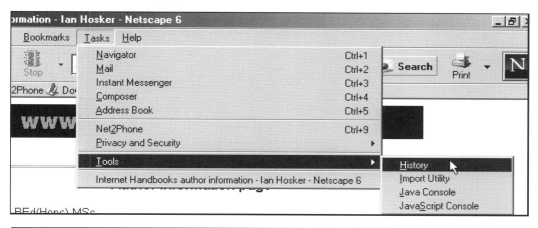

Figure 2.19. In Netscape, the URLs of sites visited are listed in the History window.

Creating bookmarks

The problem with the History function is that it is a temporary record. After a predetermined period a record of an individual page visited will be deleted. Since three weeks is the default setting for this, a site visited four weeks ago will not be available to you via History.

There is a permanent way of recording a web site so that it can be visited again at any time in the future. This assumes that the site is still available, of course.

Internet Explorer
If you have located and are viewing a site that you believe is valuable to you, select **Favorites** from the tool bar. This will open a sidebar listing bookmarked sites (figure 2.20). Click the Add button to open the Add Favorite dialog box. This box provides a default name for

Visiting web sites ....

Figure 2.20. Internet Explorer. Like the page you are currently viewing? Bookmark it! Click the Favorites button on the tool bar to open the Bookmarks list.

Figure 2.21. Internet Explorer. Click the Add button to open the Add Favorite box. Clicking OK will add a shortcut to this page in the Bookmarks list.

Figure 2.22. In Netscape, bookmarking the page you are currently viewing is done through the Bookmarks menu.

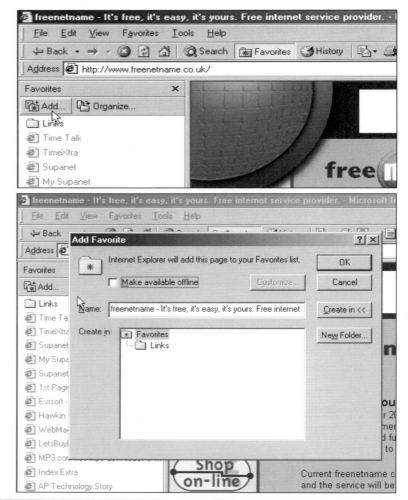

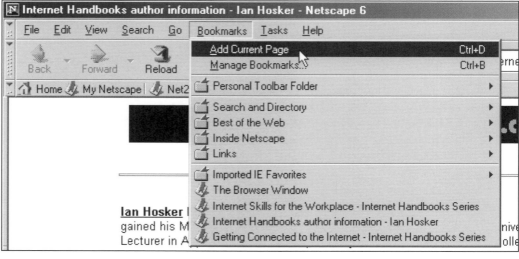

the page you want to bookmark. You can change this by typing another name in the Name box (figure 2.21). Click Ok to add the page reference and URL to Favorites.

Netscape
Select Bookmarks on the menu bar, and then Add current page (figure 2.22). This will add the page URL and page description to the bottom of your Bookmarks menu.

Using a bookmark to visit a site

Internet Explorer
Click Favorites on the tool bar to open the Favorites sidebar. Simply select the page link you want and it will automatically load (figure 2.23). You can close the sidebar by clicking on the X at the top right-hand corner of the sidebar (figure 2.24).

Figure 2.23. Internet Explorer. To revisit a bookmarked page, select it from the Favorites list.

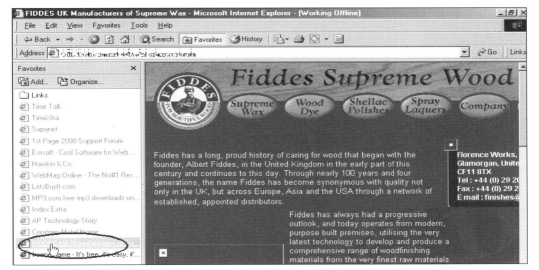

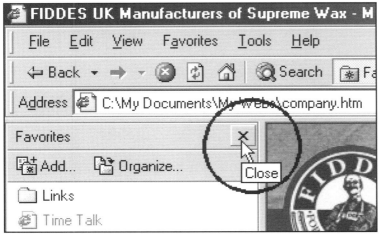

Figure 2.24. In Internet Explorer, X closes the bookmarks list.

Visiting web sites ....

Figure 2.25. Netscape. To revisit a bookmarked page, select it from the list in the Bookmarks menu.

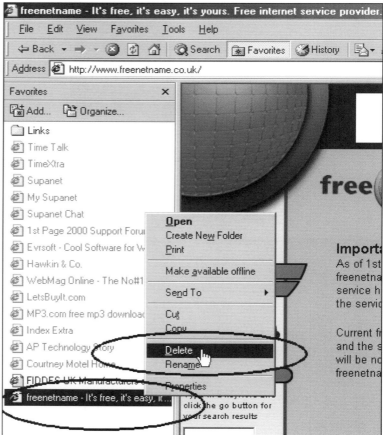

Figure 2.26. Internet Explorer. Deleting a redundant bookmark.

Netscape
Select Bookmarks from the menu bar. Select the page reference you want from the list at the bottom of the menu (figure 2.25). The browser will seek and load the page.

Deleting bookmarks

As you continue to add bookmarks, the list will continue to grow. Some bookmarks may outlive their usefulness. In this case they can be deleted, to reduce clutter. This is an easy process.

Internet Explorer

(a) Open the Favorites sidebar as described earlier in the section Creating Bookmarks.

(b) Point to the bookmark you want to delete and press the right hand mouse button once to open a short menu. Select Delete from the menu to remove the bookmark (figure 2.26).

Netscape

1. Select Bookmarks from the menu bar, and then Manage Bookmarks. This will open the Manage Bookmarks window (figure 2.27).

2. Select the bookmark to be deleted, and press the Delete button on your keyboard.

Figure 2.27. Netscape. Deleting a redundant bookmark.

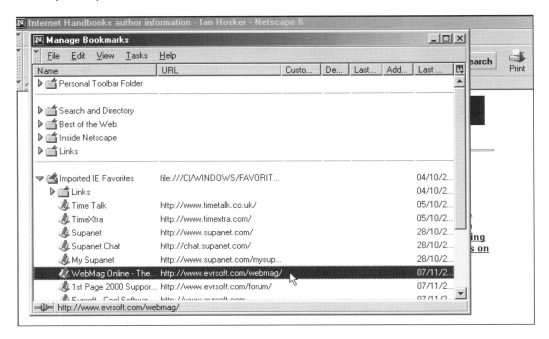

39

Visiting web sites ....

Can I keep the information once I have found it?

So far, this chapter has considered the process of visiting and navigating your way around web sites. It has shown how to use your computer's ability to record your browsing history to revisit sites of particular value. But the whole point of visiting web sites is to find information and perhaps keep a permanent record of it. This is an example of the business research function of the internet. A permanent record of such information could be very useful to you.

Printing a web page

Figure 2.28. The 'print' button on the tool bar is a quick way to print the web page you are currently viewing.

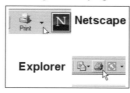

The most obvious way to keep a permanent copy of a web page is to print it. Browser tool bars have a printer symbol (figure 2.28). Click on this symbol (icon) to operate your printer. Your printed copy will include text and images as seen on the screen.

Saving web pages

An important point to consider is the cost of browsing. Unless you are with a largish company where the computer network effectively has a permanent connection to the internet, lengthy browsing can push up the daytime phone bills. However, this cost can be minimised easily. There are two ways to ensure you have a copy of sites visited on your computer. Both enable you to view the pages while offline – that is, while the browser is open but not connected to the Internet.

Printing while online takes time and so will cost. It is much cheaper to print a copy of a page you have saved on your computer's hard disk rather than directly from the internet. Internet Explorer enables you to save a web page complete with images (Netscape will only save the textmatter).

Make sure that a page has been completely loaded into your browser before you try to save a copy.

Internet Explorer

1. Select File from the menu bar, and Save As from the menu. This will open the Save As dialog box (figure 2.29).

2. The Name box will give the file a name by default. Accept or change this as you wish. The 'Save as type' box should read Web Page, complete (*.htm,*html). This means that the page will be saved exactly as viewed on screen, including images.

3. Select the location you want to save the page to, then click Save.

Netscape

1. Select File from the menu bar, and then 'Save page as' from the menu.

2. Accept or change the name of the file as you wish. Then select the location you want to save the file to in the Save File dialog box. Now click Save (figure 2.30)

Figure 2.29. Internet Explorer enables you to save a web page complete with its images.

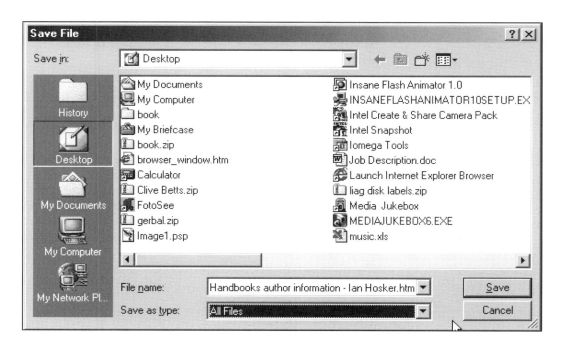

Figure 2.30. Netscape will not let you save images when you save a web page. Only the text and its layout can be saved.

Visiting web sites ....

Tutorial

The activities in this tutorial will help you gain practice in the skills described in this chapter.

Navigating a site
1. Visit the home page of Internet Handbooks (http://www.inter-net-handbooks.co.uk).
2. Save a copy of this page in your My Documents folder.
3. Use the appropriate link on this page (Site Index) to find author information on Ian Hosker.
4. Save a copy of this page in your My Documents folder.
5. Use the appropriate link to view the online catalogue.
6. Save this page in your My Documents folder.
7. Return to the home page using the back/forward arrows on the *tool bar.*
8. Bookmark this page and check that it has been added to the list of Bookmarks (Netscape) or Favorites (Internet Explorer).
9. Close down your browser.

Using History and bookmarks
1. Open your web browser, and connect to the internet if the dial-up dialog box appears.
2. Use your browser's History function to return to the author information page on Ian Hosker.
3. Use the back arrow to return to your browser's start page.
4. Use the Favorites (Explorer) or Bookmarks (Netscape) menu to return to the Internet Handbooks home page. If a reference to this page is not in the menu list, then you did not successfully complete step 8 in the previous exercise.

Viewing and printing pages offline
1. In the first exercise you saved a number of web pages. Use Windows Explorer to see the list of saved pages in the My Documents folder. Double-click on one of these pages to view it (your default web browser will open automatically to display the page without going online).
2. Print the page.
3. Repeat the process for the remaining pages.

▶ *Note* – If you use Netscape, you will not be able to view or print images that should be part of the page because this particular browser does not save images.

Your learning outcomes checklist

At the beginning of the chapter you were given a list of things you should know or be able to do by the time you had worked through the chapter. These learning outcomes are listed again for you to consider. Use the checklist as a self-assessment tool to see if you can confidently say you have achieved them. Where you feel that you have not achieved a learning outcome, or would like to have another go to make sure, you are given a pointer to the section to revisit.

Outcome	Achieved?	If not, or want to recap, revisit
Know how a web site address is structured.		What is a web site address?
Know what a web browser does.		What are the features of a web browser?
Understand the purpose of each of your browser's features.		What are the features of a web browser?
Be able to use the web browser to visit a web site using its address.		How can I access an organisation's web site?
Be able to revisit sites using the 'history' facility.		Is there an easy way to revisit sites?
Be able to use 'bookmarks'.		Is there an easy way to revisit sites?
Know how to save web pages to view 'off-line' and to print them.		Can I keep the information once I have found it?

3 Using search engines

In this chapter, we will explore:

▶ *learning outcomes for this chapter*
▶ *what is a search engine?*
▶ *how does a search engine work?*
▶ *how do I set up a keyword search?*
▶ *how do I make a category/directory search?*
▶ *what if my search results don't match what I am looking for?*
▶ *redefining your searches*
▶ *are all search engines the same?*
▶ *tutorial*
▶ *your learning outcomes checklist*

. . . .

Learning outcomes for this chapter

You know what information you need, but have no idea of where to find it. In this chapter you will learn how to use the internet as a research tool – finding information using search engines. By the end of the chapter you will:

1. Be able to describe the term **search engine**.

2. Understand what a search engine does.

3. Understand what is meant by **search criteria**.

4. Be able to use simple and complex search criteria to find web sites.

5. Understand that there are differences between search engines.

6. Know you can select different search engines for specific purposes.

7. Be able to use the internet to gather and present information on any given topic.

What is a search engine?

If you do not know the URL of an organisation or individual's web site, and you cannot guess it, you will need to use a search engine. A search engine is also needed if you are searching for web sites that will give you information on a specific subject of interest to you. In this case, you are not likely to be interested in a particular site, but will want to find information from a variety of sources, or will want to find the 'best' site for the information.

▶ A *search engine* – can be described simply as a database of individual web sites and their component pages. As with any conventional database, information is stored and can be retrieved on demand according to a set of search criteria. These are instructions to search the database for records that conform to your criteria. For example, if a company keeps a database of customers that lists and describes each customer's details. It would then be possible to set up a search request based on, for example, customers who placed orders for a particular product. The database would then set out to identify all records of customers matching the criterion, and will create a list for viewing or printing.

▶ *Internet search engines* – do the same task. They are web sites that give the visitor access to a massive database of web pages that act as a resource for anyone wanting information on a given topic. In fact, it is the presence of these web sites that makes the Internet a valuable research tool.

It is also worth noting that many large or complex sites operate an **internal search engine** which the visitor can search for something specific. Typical examples of this will be companies who operate online shopping or trading.

▶ *Example* – You could search a packaging company's site for specific type of packaging you need for your product. The internal search engine would then create a list of references to pages of products that you can then view. This prevents the visitor from having to trawl through large areas of the web site that are of no interest.

How does a search engine work?

Search engines are both proactive and reactive in the way the database is built up. The creator of a web site will want as many people as possible to visit it. One way of doing this is to register the site with as many search engines as possible. Once registered, the search engine software will seek out the site, analyse the content of its pages and record the details. Many engines will classify a site under one of many subject groupings – a sort of web directory. Figure 3.1 shows the home page of the Yahoo! search engine. A web site that provides this gateway to categories of web sites is called a **portal.**

The engine can be used in one of two ways:

▶ *keyword search* – typing in a word or phrase in the search criterion box.

▶ *directory search* – the search engine's main page lists categories of entries in its database. You can search through a category, rather than set up a specific keyword search.

Using search engines...

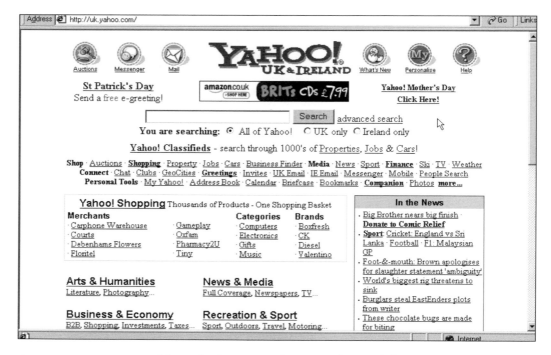

How do I set up a keyword search?

To search for information using a search engine you will need criteria to search by. The basic method is to use a **keyword**. This is a single word that is likely to be found on web pages containing the information you want. It is described as a keyword because of its strong association with the required information.

Method 1

For example, if you are looking for a possible supplier of packaging for your organisation's products, you might use 'packaging' as the keyword. This is because you would expect to find that word in web pages of packaging suppliers. For the purpose of illustration, the Yahoo! search engine will be used to search on packaging.

1. To start a keyword search, it is best to plan your search session before you connect to the Internet. This is because the process can be a hit-or-miss affair as the keyword you intend to use may not yield the results you want, or may produce too long a list of 'hits' – several million hits is not unusual! Draw up a list of possible keywords associated with the information you are looking for, e.g. packaging, containers, boxes, etc.

2. Open your web browser and make sure you are connected to the Internet. In the address bar, type www.yahoo.co.uk (the URL of Yahoo!) then press the Enter key on your keyboard.

3. Type your keyword in the search box, as shown in figure 3.2. Note that there are other options that allow you to search its database of pages across the whole web, or to search only on UK sites. This is a useful way of focusing your search because you are more likely to want to identify UK based suppliers of packaging. So, click on the UK option and then on the Search button.

Figure 3.2. Use the search criterion box to type in your keyword.

4. The search engine will now interrogate its database for all references to your keyword and build a list of pages containing the word (see figure 3.3). At the top of the list you can see how many pages it has found. Below that you will see a list of references to web pages in blue. These are links to groups of web pages. Clicking on a link will take you to that group.

Figure 3.3. The search results page, showing links to web pages, or groups of web pages. The first link is circled. There are 28 matches altogether.

5. The group of pages are shown as a series of links to specific packaging company web sites (figure 3.4).

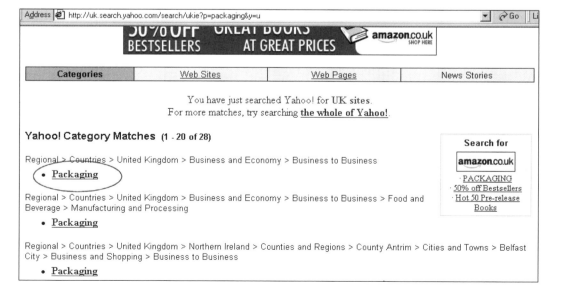

Using search engines..

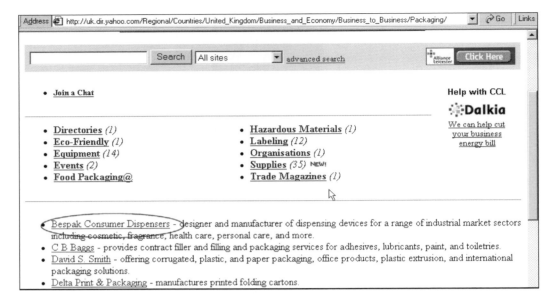

Figure 3.4. What you are really looking for are links to specific web sites – an example is circled.

6. You can visit other pages by selecting from the list and returning to the list afterwards using the *Back* arrow on the browser's tool bar.

7. There is a limit to the number of references the search engine can display on a page. If you scroll down to the bottom of the page, you will see a button that allows you to move to the next page of references (see figure 3.5).

Method 2

The second method searches in exactly the same way, but you use the browser's Search facility directly from the tool bar (see figure 3.6). Internet Explorer and Netscape both have this facility. It provides a shortcut to a search engine, and creates a side panel in which to carry out your search. You simply carry out your searches using the search engine shown in the side panel.

Figure 3.5. Clicking the next group of matches button (circled) moves you to the next page of the search results list.

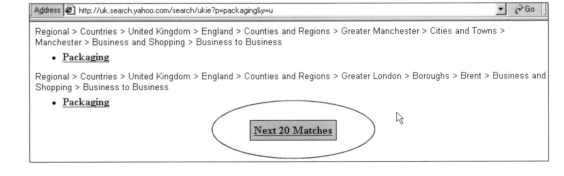

Figure 3.6. Clicking the Search button on the browser tool bar opens a search engine in a side panel of your browser window.

How do I make a category/directory search?

Search engine sites tend to classify their database entries into a series of categories. These categories are listed on the site's home page as a series of links to each category (see figure 3.7).

Each category is made up of a hierarchy. You work your way through the categories until you finally end up with a list of individual sites. It is a process where you start with a generalised category (e.g. music or newspapers) and then gradually work sequentially towards a much narrower sub-category that best matches your requirements.

Figure 3.7. Most search engines enable you to search by category of site (News and Media is circled as an example).

Using search engines . . . .

Figures 3.8 to 3.11 show the sequence of results using this approach when looking for newspapers.

1. Click on the **News & Media** (circled in figure 3.7).

2. Click on the **UK Listings** link in the next window (circled in figure 3.8).

3. Click the **Newspapers** link in the next window (circled in figure 3.9). The figure next to the link represents the number of entries.

4. The next window (figure 3.10) lists links to the UK newspaper web sites in the Yahoo! database.

5. Clicking on a link will take you to the newspaper's web site – the Barnsley Chronicle, in this case (figure 3.11).

There is one major problem with this type of search: it can lead you down a 'blind alley'. It is a fairly crude approach to searching the internet for specific information. On the other hand, it can be a quick route to finding general information on, say, university web sites or newspapers and journals.

What if my search results don't match what I am looking for?

A simple keyword search may be enough to call up the information you need, but more often than not, you wil end up with a very long list of links to pages that have, at best, a tangential link.

For example, suppose you are trying to find a hotel for a business trip to Manchester; using 'hotel' as the keyword – even if you specify a search on UK references only – will lead to a huge list. It would be very useful if you could be more specific than that. You can, thanks to something called **Boolean logic**, named after a nineteenth-century British mathematician called George Boole.

Figure 3.8. Category searches lead you through a series of sub-categories.

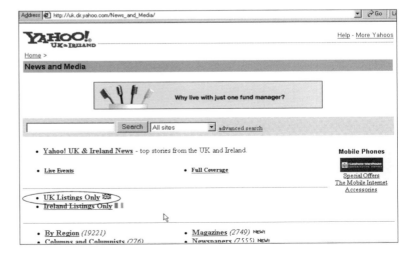

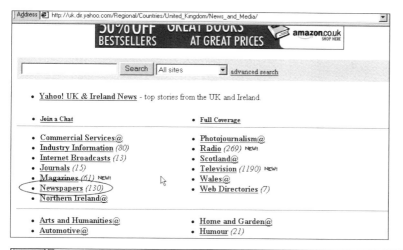

Figure 3.9. Sub-categories become more specific as you move through the hierarchy.

Figure 3.10. Categories ultimately lead to links to individual web sites.

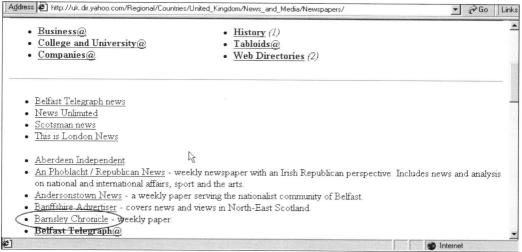

Figure 3.11. so you can eventually find the entry for the Barnsley Chronicle!

Using search engines . . . .

Boolean logic

This technique allows you to string together keywords and phrases to narrow down the list of results. The method works because the search engine database obeys a set of rules that underpin Boolean logic. For example, you can use Boolean logic to create a specific search on hotels in Glasgow. (Note: it will pick up hotels with Glasgow in the name also, and these will not necessarily be based in that city.) Nevertheless, instead of getting a list of tens of thousands, you will get a more manageable list of tens or hundreds, ranked in order of best match. This can still result in a dauntingly long list, but shorter than it would be otherwise.

As with straight keyword search criteria, you may need to experiment with combinations of keywords liked together in different ways. Keywords linked together like this are called **strings**.

The Boolean logic rules

Table 3.1 lists the more common rules for advanced searching. Individual *search engines* do provide some help by allowing you to create a more advanced search. Yahoo! for example has an Advanced Search button that allows you to specify how multiple keywords should be processed.

Rule	Use	What it does
" "	"four star hotel"	Will only pick up pages where this exact phrase is present.
AND	hotel AND Glasgow	Will identify web pages that have both *hotel* and Glasgow in the text.
NOT	cat NOT siamese	Use this to exclude a word from the results. Cat NOT Siamese should produce references to pages with cat but not of the Siamese variety! This needs to be used carefully, as you might also exclude useful pages simply because of a single reference to the unwanted keyword.
OR	colour OR color	Useful where there are alternative words or spellings of words.
( )	("four star hotel") AND Manchester	The brackets allow you to construct more complex search phrases. In this case, the returned list should be quite short and will have the phrase "four star hotel" and "Manchester" on the page or embedded in its source code.

Table 3.1. Advanced search rules – Boolean logic.

Type the search **string** in the search criterion box as you would a single keyword, and select the search button as previously described. Figure 3.12 shows this Boolean logic being used to carry out a more advanced search for hotels in Glasgow. Figure 3.13 shows the result of that search using Yahoo!

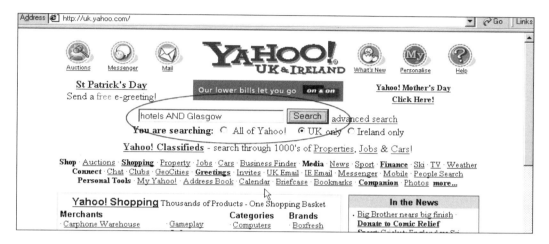

Figure 3.12. A simple Boolean logic keyword search should reduce the number of hits and so generate more relevant search results.

Figure 3.13. Effective searching has created a list of only ten – an easily managed list to search through.

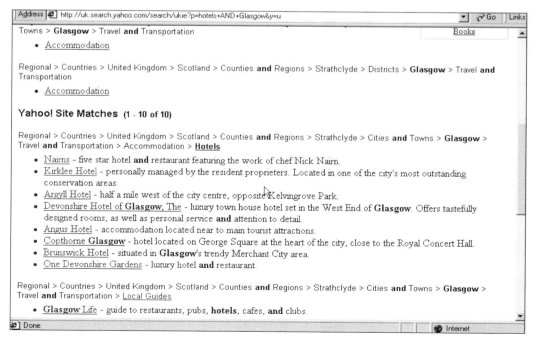

Redefining your searches

Inexperienced search engine users often find searching for information very frustrating. They end up with result listings which are literally thousands (even millions) of entries long. Also, the ones that appear near the top of the list bear no relationship to what they want. Even experienced users can get frustrated! The difference is that experienced users tend to know the wrinkles and are better prepared for redefining search criteria.

Choosing keywords
Early in the chapter, we suggested you do some initial preparation for a search session by drawing up a list of likely keywords. The same applies to advanced searches using Boolean logic strings. Try to think of possible string combinations before you call up a search engine. Then, if you are frustrated by one string, you can try another, and another, and so on.

Troubleshooting
If you cannot find the information you want, there are several likely causes:

1. Your search criteria are not specific enough.

2. The search engine's database does not contain any entries that are a close match to your search criteria.

3. There is no information on the internet that closely matches your requirements.

The third option is not likely when you consider the sheer volume of web pages – but it is possible .
   The first is often the main culprit, which is why this chapter advises being very specific and sophisticated in your use of search criteria.
   The second option – a gap in the search engine's database – is also possible. For example, you may have specified that the search should only cover part of the search engine's database, such as UK sites only. If this does not yield any suitable results, it may be worth redefining your search to include the entire database. Even then, the results list may be way off beam for you.
   Just because you can't find that all-important piece of information does not necessarily mean it is non-existent. No database is infallible. Search engines collate their information from a range of sources. They are also dependent on web authors, called **webmasters**, for registering their sites with the search engine. The search engine will then visit the site and catalogue its pages. No two search engine databases are identical.

Are all search engines the same?

All search engines are not the same. Their databases differ, sometimes greatly so. A search on two engines using the same keyword or string will always generate different results. If you fail to find what you want with one search engine, it is a good idea to try another. If you are researching a subject in detail, and are looking for information from as wide a range of sources as possible, use more than one search engine. The content of most will to a lesser or greater degree overlap, but the value of this approach lies in picking up the differences.

As you gain experience in the use of search engines, their individual characteristics, strengths and weaknesses will become familiar to you. Many regular users select particular engines for a given purpose. For example, if the information you want is likely to be found on a UK based site, it will be more efficient to use one of the UK content search engines (see table 3.2).

The differences in results listings arise from several factors:

1. Some search engines are more proactive than others in scanning the internet for web sites.

2. The way that search engines index or catalogue web pages in the database differs – so they will react differently to particular keywords or search strings.

3. Search engines rely on webmasters (web site authors) submitting their sites to them for inclusion. A site may simply not have been submitted to some engines.

4. Some search engines are specialised, dealing only with specific categories of site. Others limit themselves to particular countries.

Who's who among the search engines
Table 3.2 lists and describes the main general search engines.

Tutorial

In these exercises, you are asked to find, print and collate information. This will give you practice not only in using search engines but also in summarising the results you obtain.

As a general rule, when reporting on information gathered from other sources, you should indicate the source. The information can thus be checked again. This can present a problem when working with web sites. It is quite common for web site material to be updated, changed, moved, or even removed from the internet altogether. Still, it is important to use the discipline of recording your source(s) of information.

Using search engines..

Search engine	URL	Description
Alta Vista	www.altavista. digital.com	Another large search engine and web directory.
Ask Jeeves	www.ask.co.uk	This is one of a relatively new breed of engines that search other engines and list the best matches. An efficient way of using the resources of lots of search engines in one search.
Google	www.google.com	Combines a search engine and directory.
Hotbot	www.hotbot.co.uk	Search engines and web directories whose content is essentially UK based.
Infoseek	www.infoseek.co.uk	
Ixquick	www.ixquick.com	
Lycos	www.lycos.co.uk	One of the first.
Search UK	www.searchuk.co.uk	UK oriented.
UK Plus	www.ukplus.co.uk	UK oriented.
Yahoo!	www.yahoo.com www.yahoo.co.uk	A good general search engine. The co.uk site has a UK bias. As these sites also provide the main news headlines and stories of the day, the UK version is useful.

Table 3.2. General search engines.

Try your hand at the following:

1. I need to make a business trip to Lake Taupo in New Zealand. I want to keep the costs down, so find me a list of motels and the costs of staying for 6 nights.

2. The **Regulation of Investigatory Powers Act 2000** (sometimes called RIP) will prove to be quite important to my UK business. Someone told me there is a site that publishes the full text of the Act. Find the site and either save or print out a full copy of the Act (see chapter 1 for instructions on how to save web pages).

3. Produce a list of hotels in Sidmouth, Devon, and include their tariffs where that information is given.

4. I am about to start a new business making reproduction furniture. It is important that I have up-to-date advice on safety regulations relating to woodworking machinery and the workshop environment. Produce a list of information sources that will help me.

5. I want to start a business creating 'natural' cosmetics. Find me a list of possible suppliers who will supply relatively small quantities of raw materials by mail order.

These are quite challenging exercises, so allow yourself plenty of time!

Your learning outcomes checklist

At the beginning of the chapter you were given a list of things that you should know or be able to do by the time you had worked through the chapter. These learning outcomes are listed again for you to consider. Use the checklist as a self-assessment tool to see if you can confidently say you have achieved them. Where you feel that you have not achieved a learning outcome, or would like to have another go to make sure, you are given a pointer to the section to revisit.

Outcome	Achieved?	If not, or want to recap, revisit
Be able to describe the term 'search engine'.		What is a search engine?
Understand what a search engine does.		What is a search engine? How does a search engine work?
Understand what is meant by search criteria.		How does a search engine work? How do I set up a keyword search?
Be able to use simple and complex search criteria to find web sites.		How do I set up a keyword search? What if my search results don't match what I am looking for?
Understand that there are differences between search engines.		Redefining searches. Are all search engines the same?
Know you can select different search engines for specific purposes.		Are all search engines the same?
Be able to use the internet to gather and present information on any given topic.		Tutorial – but you may also need to revisit other parts of this chapter for specific help.

Using search engines ....

More Internet Handbooks to help you

▶ *Search Engines on the Internet*, Kye Valongo (Internet Handbooks). Search engines: a practical illustrated guide to what they are, where to find them, how they work, and how to use them effectively,

▶ *Where to Find It on the Internet*, Kye Valongo (Internet Handbooks, 2nd edition). An illustrated guide to the top web sites for all education, leisure, and the world of work.

See back cover for contact details, or visit the Internet Handbooks web site: www.internet-handbooks.co.uk

4 Business communications: the email revolution

In this chapter, we will explore:

▶ *learning outcomes for this chapter*
▶ *what is email?*
▶ *what does email look like?*
▶ *can I send and receive business documents with email?*
▶ *is the email system secure?*
▶ *what is netiquette?*
▶ *your learning outcomes checklist*

. . . .

Learning outcomes for this chapter

This chapter looks at how email has revolutionised business communications. It looks at what email technology can do for the effective running of a business. The early part of this chapter assumes you are new to the world of email. If you have some experience, you may want to start reading from the question: **Can I send and receive business documents with email?** By the end of this chapter you will:

1. Have an understanding of email technology.

2. Have an understanding of what you can do with email.

3. Have an understanding of how to exchange business documents by email.

4. Understand the principles of internet security.

5. Understand the basic principles of 'netiqette'.

What is email?

Email, or electronic mail, is now one of the easiest ways to communicate with people. Unlike faxes, it is not intrusive because you are able to exert some measure of control over sending and receiving messages. You can email a colleague at the next desk to you (provided both computers are part of an office computer network) or a customer on the opposite side of the world. It is a cheap and quick form of communication.

First, you compose a message using **email software**. Then you address the message to the intended recipient (for this you need to know their email address). When you are satisfied that the message

is complete, you instruct the software to 'send' it. It is very like composing a business memo. The document usually looks rather like a business memo on screen, so if you have experience of word processing, it should have a familiar feel.

Email programs

You will need a dedicated email program on your computer. So will the people to whom you will send emails. There are many such programs available so it is likely that many recipients of your messages will be using a different program to you. Luckily, this is not usually a problem. Unlike most other types of software, there is a high degree of compatibility among email programs..

Suppose you create a word-processed document and want to send it on disk to someone else, a client for example. You will need to check that the client is using the same program, or that your document is saved in a format that can be opened by the recipient's software. This can be a hassle, of course. Email programs do not suffer from this inconvenience, otherwise the whole technology would be pointless. You can compose and send email confident that the recipient will be able to read its contents.

This book has focused on the use of Microsoft's Internet Explorer and on Netscape for browsing. Both programs have accompanying email software, and the following chapters will concentrate on those. If you are using a different email program, don't worry too much because much of what will be described is generic. Email programs, like web browsers, work along very similar lines. The following chapters will describe the use of:

(a) Microsoft's Outlook, and its cut down version Outlook Express.

(b) Netscape's Messenger.

The reason these have been chosen is that they are by far the most commonly used email programs.

▶ If you use Internet Explorer as your browser, you will also have Outlook Express or Outlook as your email program.

▶ If your browser is Netscape, then Messenger will almost certainly be your email program. Netscape differs from Microsoft in that it has integrated its Navigator browser and Messenger programs so that you can easily switch from one application to the other from the program's menu bar.

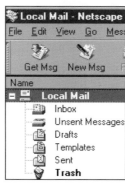

Microsoft has opted to keep its browser (Internet Explorer) and email programs (Outlook or Outlook express) as separate applications.

Outlook and Outlook Express

Before continuing, here is a quick word about the difference between

Outlook and Outlook Express. The full Outlook program is part of Microsoft's Office suite. It is a highly sophisticated personal organiser program. It has a range of built in applications, such as an appointment calendar.

Outlook Express, on the other hand, is a much simpler program. It is designed solely for the purpose of emailing. It is bundled together with Internet Explorer. When you install the Internet Explorer software, Outlook Express is also installed on your computer.

Outlook is a good business application, while Outlook Express is perfect for the home user.

Email addresses

As well as an email program, you also need a 'location' – an email address that identifies you as a possible recipient of email messages. Also, if you want to send an email to someone, they need to have an email address as well. What is more, you need to know your recipient's address, and a sender needs to know yours. You can see why it is called 'mail'. The underlying principle is the same.

The form of the email address is very much linked to the URL of the organisation's, or individual's, web site. For example, if the URL of the Acme Cosmetics Company is www.acme.co.uk, the email address of Joe Soap, it's chief buyer, will reflect this. His email address may take one of several forms. Here are four such possible addresses:

joesoap@acme.co.uk	J.Soap@acme.co.uk
jsoap@acme.co.uk	Joe@acme.co.uk

The key features are the unique domain identifier @acme.co.uk, which is taken from the URL, and the unique person identifier, which is placed before the @ in the address. In other words, the email address is unique to the individual. No one else in the world will have this address! Even if there are 2,000,000 Joe Soaps in this world, this address is unique to that Joe Soap who works for Acme Cosmetics. Of course, if there are two Joe Soaps at Acme, a little ingenuity is required. Perhaps their individual addresses could be:

jsoap.sales@acme.co.uk

and

jsoap.labs@acme.co.uk

This may be cumbersome, but at least the two individuals are uniquely identifiable by their email addresses!

Email addresses do not have to be restricted to human beings. Many organisations, too, have generic addresses for departments or functions within the organisation. For example, the sales department at Acme Cosmetics could have the following email address:

sales@acme.co.uk

Anyone within the sales department would be able to access mail sent to that address and process enquiries or orders sent in the message. So, while individuals may retain some degree of anonymity by this, it is obvious from the address where the sender's correspondence will end up. This is a very useful way of getting enquirers to contact your organisation, since all emails received can be categorised and automatically distributed internally to the appropriate functions without clogging up a central enquiry point.

What does email look like?

Figure 4.1. A simple email message as it looks on screen (top) and printed (bottom).

The basic email format is that of a simple text document. You can view it on screen using your email program, or print it out just like a word-processed document. Figure 4.1 shows a simple message as it would appear on screen and printed; it uses Microsoft Outlook, but there is little significant difference from other programs.

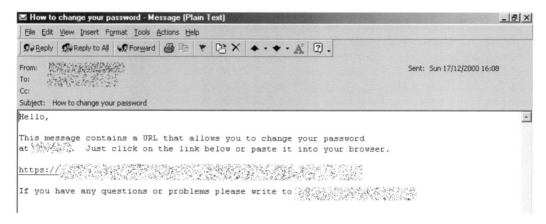

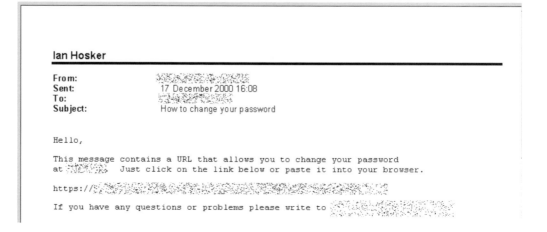

The message is made up of two parts:

▶ *Transaction details* – The details of who sent the message, the recipient, the date of transmission, and subject of the message (if the sender included one).

▶ *Message text* – This is the message itself.

The email looks just like an office memo. However, it is far more versatile than a conventional memo, as we will discover later in this and other chapters.

Can I send and receive business documents with email?

The versatility of email becomes apparent when you look at what it can do beyond the basic text transmission function. Email software enables you to send and receive business documents and other files that are **attached** to the email. For example, you can send and receive online questionnaires and forms as part of an online survey.

The email programs covered in this book allow you to send as many documents as you wish.

▶ *Example* – You have a report that must reach someone by tomorrow. Attach it to an email message and it will reach the recipient within minutes. Remember, though, your attached file is not part of the message; it is simply hitching a lift. The recipient cannot read the report directly. It is as if you sent the report on a floppy disk. The file must be opened using the appropriate program. If it is a word-processed document, it must be opened with a word processor. This will be covered in chapter 6. Chapter 5 looks at how you can send attached files via email.

The only constraint is if the recipient fails to read his or her email promptly. A quick telephone call will remedy that. But there is another potential pitfall. Your report has been written in Word 2000, but unfortunately, the recipient is using the older Word 6 – disaster! So, before sending files via email, make sure that recipients can open your files with their software. Again, a quick phone call or prior email will sort that one out. For example, you can convert your report to Word 6 format before sending it, and the recipient will then be able to open the file at the other end. Everyone is happy.

What if the document is huge?
Email programs will allow you to send any file type and size you want. However, sending massive files is not a very efficient use of email, especially if it is along a normal telephone line. The standard modem will only allow a maximum transfer rate of 56 Kbps (kilobytes per second). In reality, because of general internet traffic, the speed of

transfer (bandwidth) usually falls rather short of the maximum. This is where ISDN, ADSL and zipping (or using compressed file formats) prove invaluable.

ISDN and ADSL
ISDN stands for Integrated Services Digital Network. This technology allows for the rapid transfer of data by high-quality lines. The system copes easily with transferring large files. It requires the installation of the line into your premises and the fitting of a special piece of equipment in the computer that is connected to the line. ISDN is great for companies that have computer networks where direct internet access is available to the whole network. The normal, basic phone line could not cope with the traffic.

If you are with a graphic design company you may need to regularly transfer high specification material to your clients via electronic means. If so, ISDN, or the newer more flexible ADSL (Asymmetric Digital Subscriber Line) is the answer. Both of these technologies allow very rapid data transfer. ADSL, however, allows a much greater rate of data transfer (or bandwidth) than ISDN. The other major difference between the two technologies is the way they are designed to operate.

ISDN is, in effect, a high speed digital telephone line dedicated for the transfer of data rather than the usual speech traffic (although it can do that as well). When you want to transfer data or access the internet, the computer dials out. When you have finished, you hang up and the line closes until next time. ADSL, on the other hand has been designed to remain open at all times. In other words, your computer will be permanently connected to a 'live' terminal, 24 hours a day.

At the time of writing, several levels of service are available to suit a range of domestic and business uses of the internet and data transfer. For a fixed monthly fee, subscribers will have permanent access to the internet.

Zipping and compressed file formats
The most obvious way to reduce the time taken to transfer data over the internet is to use small files. Of course, life is never that simple. There will be times when you want to send pictures or large word-processed documents, all of which require a relatively large amount of memory. The answer lies in **compressing** the files so that they take up less memory. There are two approaches to this – using a different file format, and compressing the file.

Image files
Image files can be saved in a **file format** that considerably reduces their size. The two most widely used image formats on the internet are GIF (graphic interchange format) and JPEG or JPG (joint photographic experts group format). Most image-editing software will

save or convert images to these formats. JPEG compression is used with photo-realistic images. GIF is used to compress drawings, maps and plans. The recipient will be able to view these files using any good image-editing program. Figure 4.2 show images that are typical of each format.

Figure 4.2. Gif (top) and jpg (bottom) images. Images transferred by email are frequently sent in one of these formats.

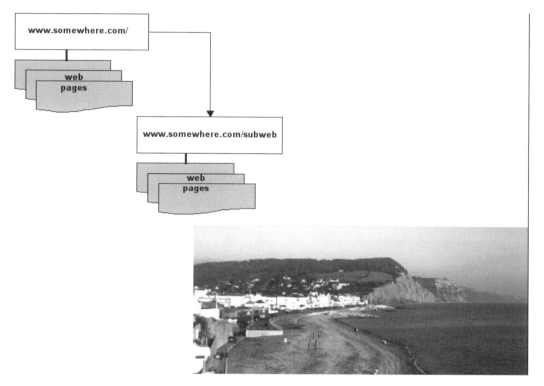

Text and number-based files

Large data files, such as detailed spreadsheets, databases and word-processed reports, require the use of a special **file compression** program. This will convert the file into something called a **zip** file. Zip files are usually considerably smaller than the original format, perhaps by as much as 70 to 90 per cent in some cases.

There is one potential flaw. The process makes the file unrecognisable by the program that originally created the file. It has to be converted back by the recipient, who must also have a zipping program. However, these programs are readily available at little or no cost. The best known of these is WinZip. Evaluation versions of WinZip (and others) are included on most of the free CDs stuck to the front of computer magazines.

Is the email system secure?

It cannot have escaped the notice of most people that there are security concerns about the use of electronic communications technology.

Business communications: the email revolution ....

These concerns fall into three main categories:

1. Hacking (or cracking). This is the process of someone 'breaking into' your computer, electronically speaking, and reading, copying or even destroying some or all of its stored data.

2. Viruses. These are small, well disguised pernicious programs sent to your computer, usually via email. They may be harmless and sent as a practical joke, but some are designed to destroy your computer's components. When sent by email, the virus will be an attached file. The main body of the email itself is safe, but if you open any attachments (see chapter 6) you may run the risk of infecting your machine (see *Anti-virus programs* below).

3. Fraud. Mostly credit card theft by someone who manages to get hold of your credit card security information from the internet.

Fortunately, these cases are relatively rare when looked at in the context of the massive volume of global internet traffic. However, if you are the victim, the rarity of the event will be of no help to you! Best practice says that you should protect yourself and your computer.

Firewalls
The firewall of a building is designed to prevent a fire spreading by blocking its path. In the same way, firewall software on a computer is designed to stop unauthorised data entering or leaving that computer when linked to the internet.

Its purpose is to defeat the attempts of hackers. When your computer – or server in the case of company networks – is connected to the internet it is 'visible', electronically speaking, to anyone else connected to the internet with the knowledge of how to find you, and so hack into your system. The risk is generally very slight if you are online for very short lengths of time, such as sending emails. Long internet sessions, however, can leave your system vulnerable. This will become more so with ADSL connections that are to all intents and purposes permanently open.

Firewall programs used to be very expensive and so were really only used with company networks, but that has changed. Quite a few programs are available for use on small networks and stand alone computers. One of the best known of these is ZoneAlarm which you can download from the developer's web site:

www.zonealarm.com

Anti-virus programs
So pernicious are virus programs that your machine can become 'infected' even if you have never had internet access. Transferring

infected files between machines on floppy disk is all it takes. This is why it is so important to install anti-virus programs on every computer. You should scan all transferred files and email attachments – even those from trusted sources.

Chapter 6 looks at how to save and open files that have been sent to you as email attachments.

▶ Best practice suggests that you should scan the attached files with your anti-virus program before opening the file. If a file is infected it should be deleted, and the sender informed. The sender may be unaware that they have an infection on their own machine.

Just as important as installing and using anti-virus software is keeping its database of known viruses up to date. There is little point installing an anti-virus program and continuing to use it in its original form for more than a couple of months. Rogue programmers are devising ever more ingenious and pernicious viruses, so the software to combat them must be kept right up to date.

Many manufacturers of anti-virus programs allow the program to connect to their web sites and download new virus recognition data. This procedure should be carried out monthly.

| Virus Alerts |
| Anti-Virus Updates |
| Virus Library |
| ▶ Virus Info Center |
| Recent Updates |
| Joke Programs |
| Trojans |
| Hoaxes |
| Web Viruses |

What is netiquette?

This is one of those awful words that form the jargon of email communication. Netiquette simply means that users should observe some basic principles of acceptable behaviour – 'internet etiquette' – with regard to the language used in emails.

Emails and written English
People often talk about the apparent negative effect of electronic communications on the quality of written English. Indeed, this is partly true. The ease and speed of communication can breed an informal language akin to conversation. However, it is unfair as a general criticism. After all, this whole new technology has actively encouraged social interaction through the written word as the effort and cost of doing so has been largely removed or reduced.

Getting the balance right
That issue aside, there is a serious point to be made about the form of language used, particularly within the business context. The speed with which email correspondence can be received and responded to can produce a semi-conversational approach. Is this approach right for a business setting? Perhaps it is, where the participants are known to each other and a degree of informality has been established between them. For new contacts, and where a communication protocol is being established, it is important to maintain a formal business language.

Business communications: the email revolution ....

Tips for composing emails

You also need to take into account that electronic communications should be quick to transmit. Messages should be economical in terms of length, so they are fast to transmit and easy to read on screen.

Here are a few pointers:

1. CAPITAL LETTERS USED LIKE THIS CAN BE INTERPRETED AS SHOUTING BY THE RECIPIENT, ESPECIALLY IF THE SENTENCE IS TERMINATED WITH EXCLAMATION MARKS!!!!!!!! As you can see the emphasis placed on the text is very marked and quite startling.

2. C U 4 T L 8 R (see you for tea later). Email just begs for the use of informal shorthand, especially if U R not O K with the keyboard. As a general rule, within a business setting the form of language really ought to mirror that used for conventional forms of written communication. Recipients will recognise and understand the meaning of formal business language. This is not to say that you can never use informal shorthand approaches, because it depends on the social relationship between you and the recipient. If it is appropriate because you have developed a good relationship where there is a high degree of informality, then use it (assuming all parties understand the language being used).

3. Long emails are tedious. Many people are not very good at reading documents on screen and will print out long emails. In general email text is not particularly attractive or suitable for conveying complex messages. It may be better to send an attachment (see chapter 5), where the material can be presented in a professional format.

4. As far as the law is concerned, an email is a published document; if you send a message which is libellous, indecent or dishonest in some way, it is treated as a publication of that material by the law. As a result you, and possibly your employer, could be liable to prosecution.

Your learning outcomes checklist

At the beginning of the chapter you were given a list of things you should know or be able to do by the time you had worked through the chapter. These learning outcomes are listed again for you to consider. Use the checklist as a self-assessment tool to see if you can confidently say you have achieved them. If you feel that you have not achieved a learning outcome, or would like to have another go to make sure, there is a pointer to the section to revisit.

Outcome	Achieved	If not, or want to recap, revisit
Have an understanding of email technology.		What is email? What does email look like?
Have an understanding of what can be done with email.		All sections.
Have an understanding of how email technology can be used to exchange business documents.		Can I send and receive business documents with email? What if the document is huge?
Understand the principles of internet security.		Is the email system secure?
Understand the underlying principles of 'netiqette'.		What is netiquette?

Internet Handbooks to help you

▶ *Getting Started on the Internet,* by Kye Valongo. An illustrated guide for absolute beginners.

▶ *Using Email on the Internet,* by Kye Valongo. An illustrated step-by-step guide to sending and receiving messages and files.

5 Composing and sending emails

In this chapter, we will explore:

▶ *learning outcomes for this chapter*
▶ *using an address book*
▶ *using Microsoft Outlook and Outlook Express for emails*
▶ *using Netscape Messenger for emails*
▶ *tutorial*
▶ *your learning outcomes checklist*

Learning outcomes for this chapter

In this chapter, you will learn the skills required to compose and send emails to colleagues, suppliers and customers. The chapter looks at three email programs that between them account for the vast majority of users: Microsoft's Outlook and Outlook Express, and Netscape's Messenger. By the end of the chapter you should be able to:

1. Set up and maintain an address book for use with your email program.

2   Compose one or more emails properly addressed.

3   Create and save emails in draft form.

4   Attach files to an email.

5   Send and receive emails via a dial-up connection.

6   Delete old emails.

Using an address book

The sections for each program begin with showing you how to use the address books associated with them. They operate just like conventional paper-based versions in that you can list the contact details of people or organisations. While not absolutely essential, they do provide you with incredibly useful tools, as you will discover throughout this chapter. You can use an address book:

▶ To store the contact details of people and organisations with whom you correspond by email.

▶ To automatically address an email to its intended recipient.

Using Microsoft Outlook and Outlook Express for emails

Outlook is a powerful personal management tool and is a component of Microsoft's Office suite. This book is only concerned with its use as an email program. Outlook Express is a cut-down version of its more sophisticated relative, but that is only because it has one function – emailing. Figure 5.1 is a view of the Outlook and Outlook Express windows.

The contents of each folder in the **Folders** window can be viewed simply by clicking on the folder name. In figure 5.1, the content of the **Inbox** can be seen. Not all the folders in Outlook are used for emailing. The **Calendar** for example acts as an appointments diary. The following is a brief description of the folders used for emails.

▶ *Inbox* – Incoming mail is stored here.

Figure 5.1. The main windows of Outlook (top) and Outlook Express (bottom).

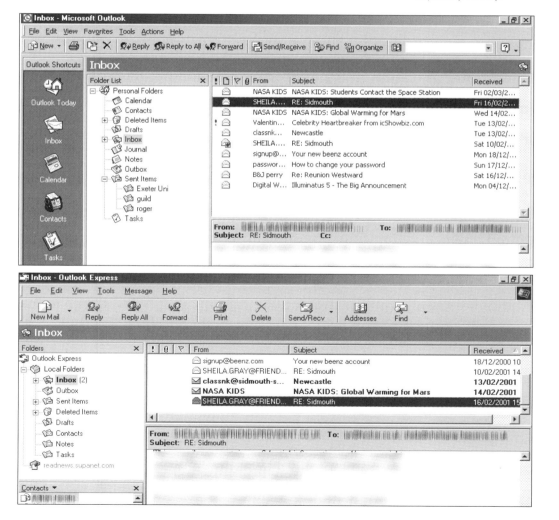

Composing and sending emails ....

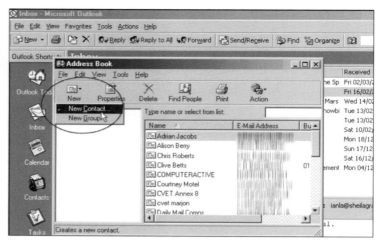

Figure 5.2. Use the Addresses button on the tool bar to open the address book to add or modify entries.

Figure 5.3. Preparing to create a new entry in the address book.

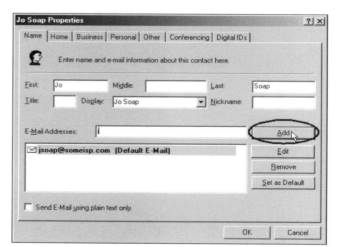

Figure 5.4. Adding the contact details of a new address book entry.

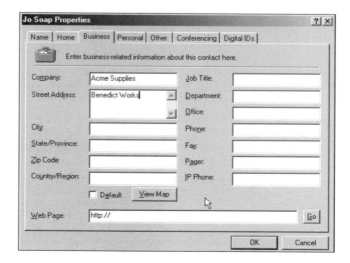

Figure 5.5. Use the remaining tabs on the Properties box to fill in other relevant details – optional!

▶ *Outbox* – Mail you send is temporarily stored here until Outlook connects to the internet.

▶ *Drafts* – Unfinished mail is stored here if it is not ready to send and you cannot complete the message in one sitting.

▶ *Sent items* – Copies of emails you send are stored here.

▶ *Deleted items* – Messages deleted from other folders are stored here.

Setting up an address book
1. To open the program's address book, position the mouse pointer over the address book icon on the tool bar (figure 5.2) and click the left hand mouse button once.

2. Once the address book window opens, click the New button on its tool bar and select New Contact from the menu (figure 5.3)

3. The contact properties box will open. Type in the details of the contact as shown in figure 5.4. After you have typed in the contact's email address in the Email Addresses box, click the Add button (circled). This will place the email address in the box below as shown in figure 5.4. As this is the only address inserted, it is labelled as the default address. People often have more than one address, so you can add as many as you like to this box by typing in the Email Addresses, clicking the Add button each time.

4. You may want to record more details about this contact, such as address and telephone numbers. The Contact Properties box has a number of tabs at the top. Figure 5.4 shows the Name area of the contacts properties in use to record email addresses. The Home, Business, Personal and Other tabs can be clicked to add more details about this contact. Figure 5.5 shows information being added to the Business section. When you have finished, click the OK button to add this contact to your address book.

Editing an address book entry
As people move on, you can edit their contact details in your address book, or delete them altogether.

1. Open the address book. If you want to delete an entry simply click on it once to highlight the entry and press the Delete button on your keyboard. You will be asked if you are sure you want to delete the entry. If you click Yes now, there will be no going back.

2. If you simply want to edit the entry, such as add a new email address or phone number, double-click on the entry. This will open the contact's details box. Edit the fields you need to and click the OK button.

Composing and sending emails ....

Creating a new Group of email addresses

There may be times when you need to email groups of people on a fairly regular basis. Perhaps you need to provide reports or other information to a sales team or a number of managers. You can set up a group of contacts and then address the email to the group. This way, you only have to address an email once and be sure that you have not left anyone out of the list.

1. Open the address book, point to and click on the File button on the menu bar and select New Group from the menu (as shown in figure 5.3).

2. The Properties gives you a number of ways of setting up the group (figure 5.6). Type in a name for the group. This will be listed in your address book for use as and when you need it, so make it recognisable.

Figure 5.6. Setting up a mailing list for email.

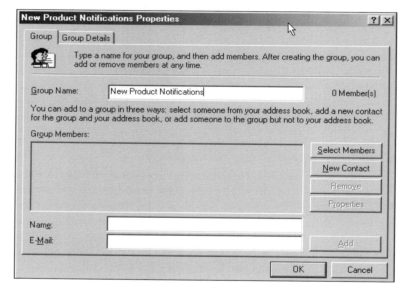

3. To add a contact already in your address book, click the select members button to open your address book. Your existing contacts are listed in the left hand box. Highlight the intended group member by clicking on the name in the box and click the Select button. The name will be added to the right-hand Members box. Repeat this exercise for all the contacts you want to include (figure 5.7). When you have finished, click OK to return to the Properties box.

4. You may want to add a new contact to the group and to your address book. Click on the New Contact button. This will open the Contact Properties box as seen in figure 5.4. Fill out the contact's details and click the OK button when you have finished. This will

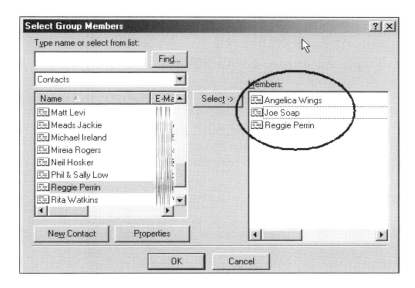

Figure 5.7. Compiling the mailing list using existing address book entries.

Figure 5.8. Adding a contact not already in your address book.

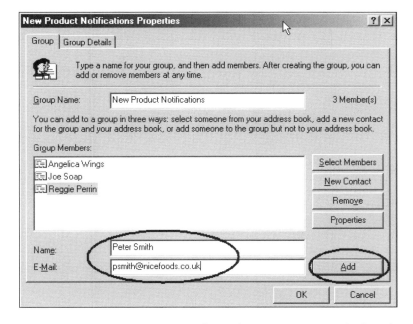

add the contact to your group list and as a separate entry in the address book. You will be returned to the Group Properties box.

5. If you want to add someone to the group who is not in your address book, and you do not want to list as a separate entry, you can type the details in the two boxes at the bottom of the Properties Box (circled in figure 5.8). Clicking the Add button will add the contact to the group membership, but will not create a separate entry in the address book.

Composing and sending emails ....

Figure 5.9. Mailing groups (lists) are clearly discernible in your address book.

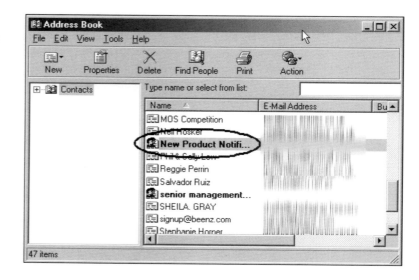

6. When the group membership has been completed, click the OK button. The group will be added to your address book (figure 5.9).

Composing an email

1. Start Outlook, or Outlook Express, if it is not already open. Make sure you have highlighted Inbox in the folders window shown in figure 5.1.

2. Click New on the menu bar. This will open a new email message window (figure 5.10). The window has a memo-like format. First you need to address the memo to one or more recipients. Then type in the subject of the email (optional), and finally compose the message in the message window.

Figure 5.10. The format of an email message is memo-like.

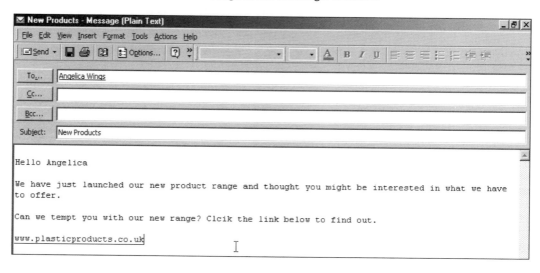

Figure 5.11. Sometimes it is quicker to type in the recipients' email addresses than look them up in the address book – but that assumes you have memorised them!

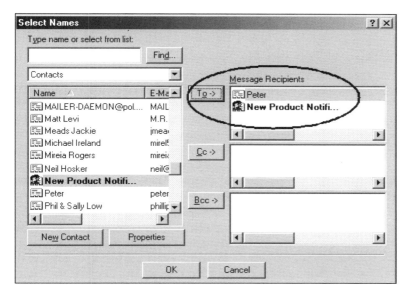

Figure 5.12. Use your address book to create a list of mail recipients.

3. To address the memo, you have two options. You can type in the email address of the recipient directly into the 'To:' text box, or use your address book (see instruction 4). If you are typing in more than one recipient, separate their addresses with a semi-colon (see figure 5.11)

4. If you want to use the address book, click the 'To:' button circled in figure 5.11. This will open the address book window. Select the addressee from the list on the left and click the 'To:' button on the right to include it in the Message Recipients list. Repeat this for everyone you want to receive the message. You can also select a group in the same way (see figure 5.12). When you have finished, click OK to return to the message window. The selected addressees will be automatically placed in the 'To:' text box.

5. If you want to give the message a subject, type that in the Subject:

text box. Type your message in the message box. You can move from box to box either using the Tab key on the keyboard, or by pointing to a box with the mouse and clicking the left-hand button to place the cursor there. See figure 5.13.

6. When you have finished your message, click the Send button at the top left-hand side of the message toolbar (see figure 5.14). This will send the message to the program's Outbox folder. You will then be returned to the Outlook or Outlook Express main window (figure 5.1). How the message then leaves your computer to wing its way to the recipients depends on the type of internet connection you have (see *How do I send my emails?*).

Can I save a draft of my email while I think about it?
There are occasions when work is interrupted at a critical point in your work on a computer. If this happens, quickly save what you have done so far, deal with the interruption, and return to the work in hand, picking up where you left off.

Emails are generally thought of as an instant form of communication. The message is written and sent in one fairly quick operation. However, you may want to prepare an email message and store it as

Figure 5.13. Giving the message a subject title is optional, but it can help the recipient identify the nature of the message when listed in their Inbox. Type the body of the message body into the lower window. Outlook (top) and Outlook Express (bottom) message windows are illustrated.

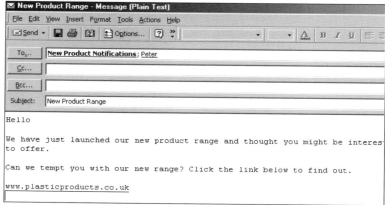

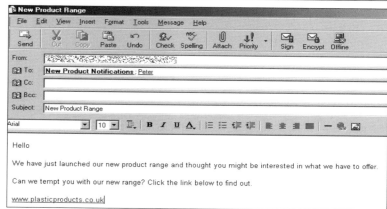

Figure 5.14. Click the Send button on the Outlook (left) and Outlook Express (right) tool bars to transmit the message.

a draft while you wait for more material to add, or give time to considering its contents. Whatever the reason, you can interrupt the creation of an email, save it as a draft, and complete the process at a later time.

(a) Create your message as described in the previous section. To save a draft, select File › Save from the menu bar (figure 5.15).

(b) The email message will remain on screen. Close the window by clicking on the 'close window' X in the top right-hand corner of the message to take you back to the Outlook main window. You should see a number 1 in blue against the Drafts folder name. The number indicates how many draft messages it contains (see figure 5.16).

(c) Later, when you want to complete the message, you can open it by clicking on the **Drafts** folder. The draft message will be listed in the upper right hand window (circled in figure 5.17). Double-click on the message to open it. You can now continue with the

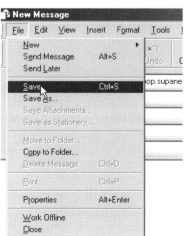

Figure 5.15. Outlook (left) and Outlook Express (right) both enable you to save a draft of your message, storing it until you are ready to finish it.

Composing and sending emails ....

Figure 5.16. The Drafts folder is holding one message in draft form.

Figure 5.17. Double-click on the draft message to open it ready for completion and transmission.

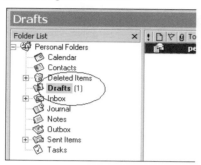

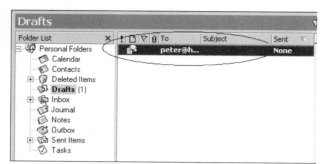

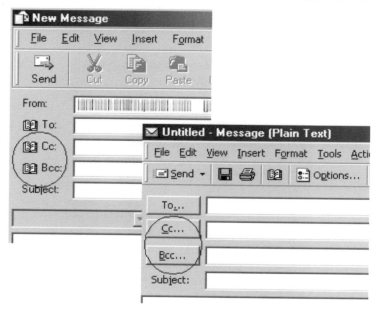

Figure 5.18. As with an office memo, you can arrange for people to receive a copy of the email message sent to a main recipient.

message. If it is complete and ready to send, click the Send button. The message window will be sent to the Outbox folder. There will not be a copy in the Drafts folder.

Sending copies of emails to someone else
It is common business practice to send a copy of a communication to other interested parties for information. You can do the same with email. When you compose a message, you will see two other boxes in the message header (figure 5.18):

1. Cc: – Adding other people's addresses to this box will ensure that a copy of the email is sent to them for information. The recipients listed in the 'To:' box will now also see that a copy has been sent to others.

80

2. Bcc: – This stands for 'blind carbon copy'. Anyone added to this box will receive a copy of the email, but the main recipients will not know – hence the term 'blind'.

Creating a new message
When you address the message, you can also determine who will receive copies. This is all done from the address book window (see **How do I compose an email?**).

From the address book window (figure 5.19), you can select people who will receive copies and blind copies by selecting the name and then pressing the 'Cc:' or 'Bcc:' buttons (circled in figure 5.19). Click OK to return to the message where all the names will be listed in the appropriate boxes.

How do I send my emails?
When you click the Send button, the message you have completed will be moved to and stored in the Outbox folder (figure 5.1). You will see a blue number in brackets next to the folder name (see figure 5.20). This represents the number of messages waiting to be sent. It is from here that the message will be transmitted to the internet for distribution. No matter how many people are listed as recipients, the message is sent only once. Your ISP's mail server will send out a copy to every recipient.

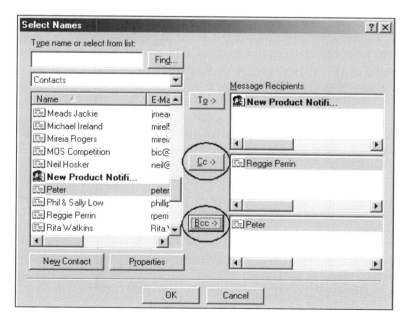

Figure 5.19. Use the address book to help you copy your message to other people.

Figure 5.20. When you send a message, it is temporarily stored in the Outbox.

Composing and sending emails ....

How and when the message is released from the Outbox to the internet depends on how your system is set up. If your system is permanently online (for example, as part of your organisation's computer network), the messages will probably be sent automatically. The blue number against the Outbox folder will disappear as the message is sent. In other words, you need do no more than click the Send button at the end of composing your message. Your computer system will do the rest.

What if I operate a dial-up connection?
If you are operating a dial-up system where the computer is not permanently online – likely if you work from home or are operating within a small business – you will have to instruct the program to go online and send any messages waiting in the Outbox.

The quickest way to go online in Outlook to send your message is to press the **F5** function button on your keyboard. Outlook will open the dial-up connection, go online, and send the messages. It will also look for any messages waiting for you on your ISP's server (see chapter 6). If you are using Outlook Express, pressing down the **Ctrl** and **M** keys at the same time will open the dial-up connection.

What if I have more than one ISP account?
Having email accounts with more than one ISP does add a slight complication. One of these accounts will be defined by Outlook or Outlook Express as the **default account** – the one it will automatically dial first if you go online. It is also the account that messages you have written will automatically be routed to when you press the Send button. If you want to send your email(s) through another of your accounts you have to tell Outlook or Outlook Express to do so:

Figure 5.21. In Outlook, you need to specify which account to use from the Menu bar.

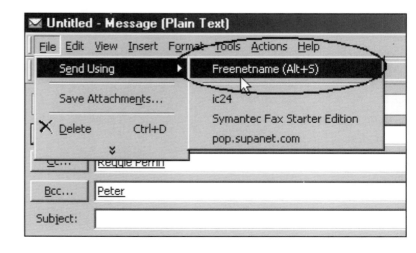

▶ *Outlook* – When you compose your email, instead of clicking the Send button, select File > Send using. from the menu bar. You can select the account to send this message through (see figure 5.21). The message will only be sent if you connect to that account through the relevant ISP. If you connect to another account, it will not be sent.

▶ *Outlook Express* – After you have pressed the Send button, your dial-up connection box will open, from which you can select the account for your connection.

Attaching files to emails

Long ago, an email was a simple text message – very like those you get on mobile phones (only longer). The ability to use email as a multi-media tool has extended its value way beyond that of simply being a messaging service. The only serious constraints are the size of the information you want to send and whether or not the recipients have the necessary software to open the files. This is discussed in chapter 4.

Figure 5.22 shows a message that is ready to have a file attached to it. You can do this at any time, but it is very easy to forget to attach the message before it is sent (the voice of experience!). If you attach the file before composing the message, this embarrassment is avoided. When you attach a file to the email, it is only a copy of the file. The original file remains intact, so when the message is sent it is the copy of the file not the original that disappears into the ether!

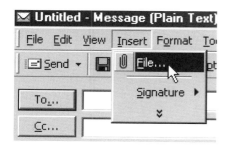 

Figure 5.22. It is a good idea to attach any files before you start composing the message – then you won't forget about them!

1. To attach the file, select either the paperclip symbol on the toolbar (circled in figure 5.22) if it is present or Insert › File (Insert › File attachment. in Outlook Express) from the menu bar. This will open the Insert File box.

2. Search for and select the file you want to attach to the email, and click the Insert button. The file will then be inserted. You will now see a little icon at the bottom of the email (circled in figure 5.23) in Outlook, or listed in the header of Outlook Express (also circled). Once the message is completed, you can send it.

Composing and sending emails ....

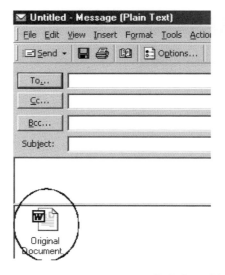

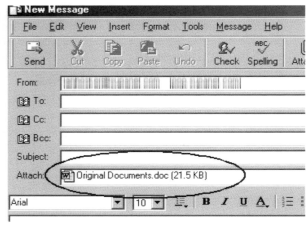

Figure 5.23. Attached files are shown as an icon at the bottom of the window in Outlook (left). They are listed in the Attach line in the Outlook Express (right) message header.

Deleting old messages

Emails are files in their own right. Just as a letter produced by a word processor is a file that becomes stored on your hard drive, so are emails. When you send an email, a copy is retained by the computer. It is stored in the Sent items folder in Outlook. If you click on the Sent items folder in the folders window of Outlook, a list of emails sent will be there. Chapter 6 looks at how you handle incoming email. Over time, the list of emails here will also grow and clutter the screen. From time to time, it is good to clear out old mail and delete it from your system. This is easy to do.

1. Select the folder you want to clear out. A list of the folder's contents will appear in the right hand window (figure 5.24). There are two options. If you simply want to delete a file from the folder,

Figure 5.24. The message delete button in Outlook Express (top) and in Outlook (bottom).

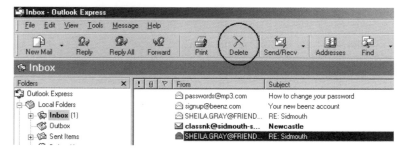

.... **Composing and sending emails**

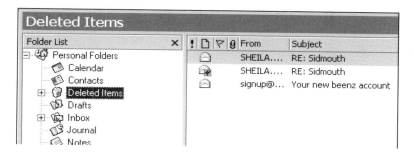

Figure 5.25. The Deleted Items folder serves the same function as the Recycle Bin in Windows.

select it in the window and either press the **Delete** button on your keyboard or click the delete button on the toolbar (circled in figure 5.24). The message will disappear. You can repeat this for each message you want to delete.

2. Actually, the messages do not disappear from the system entirely. Anything you delete from an Outlook or Outlook Express folder will be sent to the **Deleted items** folder. This has the same function as the **Recycle Bin** in windows. Select this folder in the folders window and you will see the list of messages you have apparently deleted (figure 5.25). To finally clear a message out of the system, click the delete button on the toolbar or keyboard. You will be given a warning message asking if you are sure you want to permanently delete the items. Click yes to complete the process.

Using Netscape Messenger for emails

The Netscape suite of internet programs work rather differently to those of Microsoft, not least because Netscape bundles the browsing and email programs together. If you have a dial-up connection to the internet rather than a permanent link, when you start up Netscape you will be asked to connect to the internet. This program is designed to work with a live connection to the internet, but you can cancel the dial-up connection and work offline. The browser will open and a series of icons will appear at the bottom left-hand corner of the window (figure 5.26).

Click on the **Mail** icon (circled in figure 5.26) to start Netscape Messenger. You may also find a shortcut to Messenger on the Desk-

Figure 5.26. The Mail icon at the bottom of the Netscape window is a shortcut to starting up Messenger.

Composing and sending emails ....

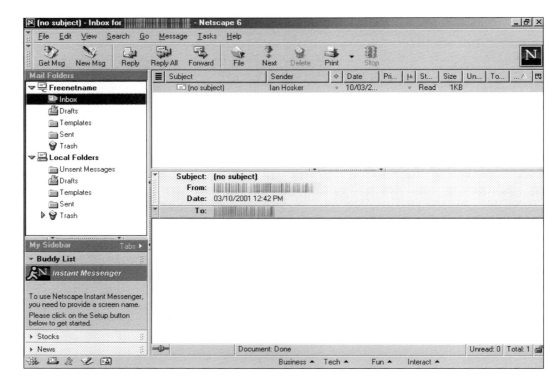

Figure 5.27. The
Messenger window.

top taskbar at the bottom of your monitor screen. The Messenger window will open (figure 5.27).

In the **Mail Folders** window you will see a set of folders. These correspond to the email accounts you have set up (one – Freenetname – in the case of figure 5.27). The **Local Folders** group is built in to the Messenger program. The following is a description of the individual folders.

1. *Inbox* – Incoming mail will be stored here. If you have more than one account, each account will have its own folder so you are able to see the source of the messages.

2. *Unsent Messages* – Mail you send are temporarily stored here until Messenger connects to the internet.

3. *Drafts* – Unfinished mail is stored here if it is not ready to send and you cannot complete the message in one sitting.

4. *Sent* – Copies of emails you send are stored here.

5. *Trash* – Messages deleted from other folders are stored here.

86

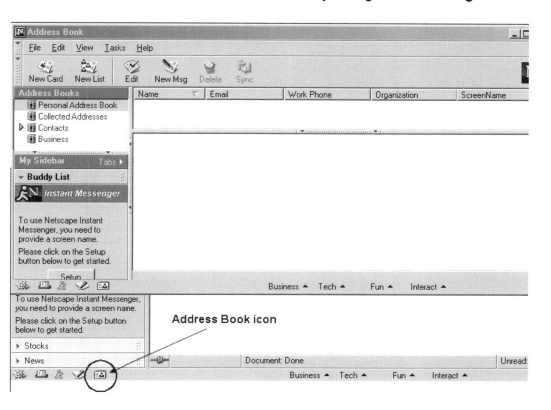

Address Book icon

Setting up an address book in Messenger

Messenger allows you to set up more than one address book. This can be pretty useful if you have a large list of possible contacts. Address books can be set up for different purposes. This section will begin by looking at how you can create a new address book before describing how to add contacts to it.

Figure 5.28. The address book icon will open Messenger's address book.

Creating a new address book

1. Click on the Address Book icon (circled in figure 5.28) at the bottom of the Messenger window. This will open the address book window (figure 5.28).

2. Select File > Address Book from the menu bar. This will open a dialog box asking you to name the new book. Type in a name and click OK. The new address book will appear in the list of books in the address book window (figure 5.29).

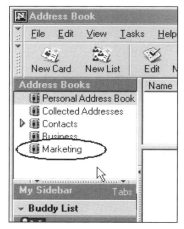

Figure 5.29. Create individual address books for specific purposes.

Composing and sending emails ....

Figure 5.30. Creating a new entry in the highlighted address book.

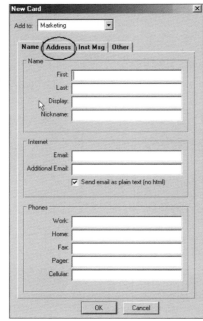

Figure 5.31. Basic contact details are entered under the Name tab. More detailed information can be stored by clicking the Address tab.

Creating a new contact
1. Click on the address book icon at the bottom left-hand corner of the Messenger window (see figure 5.28) to open the address book list. Select the address book you want to add to and click on the **New Card** icon on the toolbar menu (figure 5.30).

2. Type in the name, telephone and email contact details. If you click on the Address tab (circled in figure 5.31), you can add the mailing address of your contact as well. Click the OK button to add the contact to the selected address book.

Editing contact details
Over time, the contact details will change as people move on. You can edit or delete contact details in an address book very easily.

(a) Open the address book. If you want to delete an entry simply click on it once to highlight the entry and press the Delete button on your keyboard. There will be no going back once this action is taken.

(b) If you simply want to edit the entry, such as add a new email address or phone number, double-click on the entry. This will open the contact's details box. Edit the fields you need to and click the OK button.

Creating a mailing list
You can create a group list of people you may wish to contact regularly with information that all must have. Creating a mailing list will make this less tedious and you will not run the risk of forgetting anyone.

1. Select the address book to which you want to add the mailing list. Click the **New List** button on the address book's toolbar. This will open the **Mailing List** box (figure 5.32).

2. In the top section of the box, give the list a name (List Name). If you want, you can also add a nickname and description.

3. In the bottom section of the box, you need to type in the email addresses of the people you want to include in the list (see figure 5.33). After adding an entry to the list, press the keyboard's return key to create another entry. When you have finished the list, click the OK button.

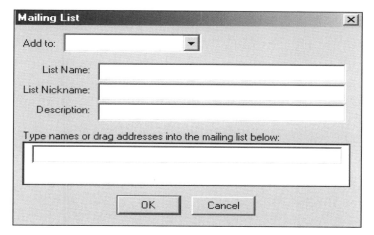

Figure 5.32. The Mailing List set up box.

Figure 5.33. Entering the details of people you want in the mailing list.

89

Composing and sending emails ....

Figure 5.34. The New Message window. Note: the header automatically displays your email address as the sender.

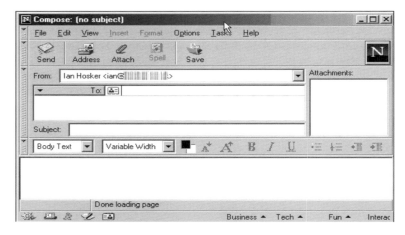

4. The mailing list will be listed in the address book's entries. You may also see some additional entries in your address book. If you added people to the mailing list who are not listed in the address book, they will be automatically added to the main address book list. A mailing list can be edited or deleted in the same way as any other entry.

Composing an email

(a) Click the **New Msg** button on the Messenger toolbar. This will open a new message window (figure 5.34).

(b) The header already includes the sender's email address. You need to address the message to someone. Click the **Address** button on the toolbar to open the address book window. Select the address book you want to use. Then select the contact or mailing list and click the 'To:' button (figure 5.35). You can add as many

Figure 5.35. Add recipients from the selected address book.

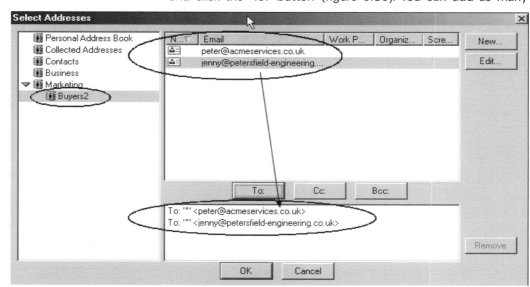

names as you like simply by repeating this process for each person you want to include. When the list is complete, click the OK button. You will be returned to the new message, which will be addressed to your intended recipients.

(c) If you make a mistake while creating the list and want to delete a recipient, simply select it in the **Select Addresses** box and click the **Remove** button (figure 5.36).

(d) Type in your message in the message window (figure 5.37).

Figure 5.36. The Remove button will delete the highlighted recipient from the recipient list.

Figure 5.37. Here is a completed email message ready to send.

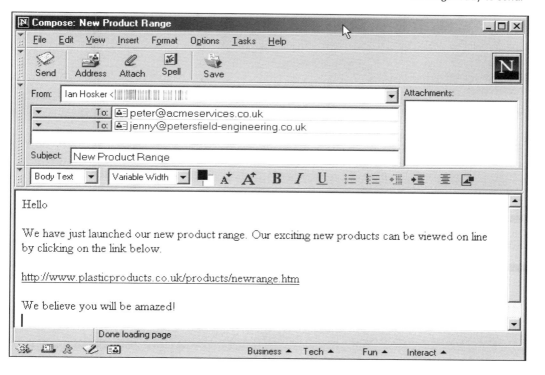

Composing and sending emails ....

Sending emails with Netscape Messenger
Once you have composed your message, how you send it depends on whether or not you are online, that is have a live connection to the internet. Netscape tends to assume you have a live connection so if you are off-line and click the **Send** button on the message tool-bar, you will get an error message saying that a connection cannot be made. The message will disappear from view, as its window will be minimised. You can open the message window again from the taskbar at the bottom of the screen.

Figure 5.38. The Send button will transmit your message if you are online.

Figure 5.39. If you are offline, use Send Later to store the message for later transmission.

Sending a message while online
If your computer has a live link with the internet, click the Send button on the message window's toolbar (circled in figure 5.38). The message will be sent and a copy will be stored in the **Sent** folder.

Sending a message later
If you composed your message while off-line, the following procedure should be adopted.

1. After completing your message, select 'File > Send later' from the menu bar of the message window (see figure 5.39).

2. The message will be stored in the **Unsent Messages** (see figure 5.40). You are now free to compose one or more other messages, which can also be stored in the **Unsent Messages** folder until such time as you want to go back online.

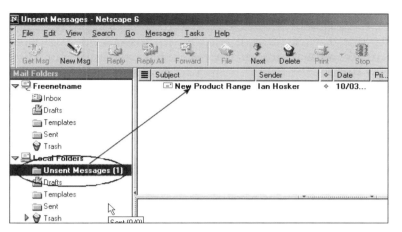

Figure 5.40. The message will be stored in the Unsent Messages folder.

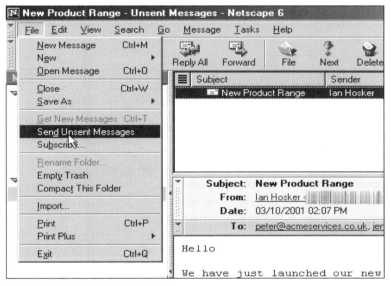

Figure 5.41. When you go online, Send Unsent Messages will transmit your stored mail.

3. This is where offline working with Netscape is awkward. You now need to close the Netscape program, then restart it. At this point you make a live connection through the dial-up connection. Open the Messenger window using the icon at the bottom left-hand side of the browser window.

4. Select 'File > Send Unsent Messages' from the menu bar (figure 5.41). Messenger will connect to the server and send your messages.

Offline working
The advantage of off-line working is that you can compose all your messages while not connected to the internet and send them all together in a single operation. Since you are not connected to the

Composing and sending emails ....

internet while composing mail, you are not paying call charges for that time. Of course, this is not an issue if you subscribe to a service offering free line time, or your organisation's network has permanent internet access via a leased line.

Can I save a draft of my email while I think about it?
Long messages, like long word-processed files, can take more than one sitting to complete. A draft of these messages can be saved, and completed and sent later.

(a) After composing as much of the message as you can or want, save a draft by selecting File › Save as › Draft from the menu bar (figure 5.42). A copy will be saved in the **Drafts** folder. You can safely close the message window.

Figure 5.42. Storing a draft of your message.

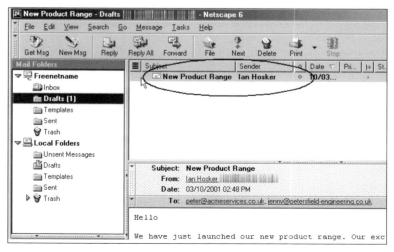

Figure 5.43. The Drafts folder will store unfinished mail. Double-click on the message you want to finish to open it for editing.

94

(b) When you are ready to finish or continue with the message, high-light the Drafts folder and double click on the message from the list in the right hand window (circled in figure 5.43). This will open the message ready for you to continue. If you finish the message, send it using the appropriate method described in **How do I send my emails?** If it needs more work, you can save it as a draft again. If you do save it as a draft again, it will create a separate message, which will be confusing because you will have a list of messages that are different versions of the same one! If possible, try to complete your message at the second sitting.

Can I copy the email to someone else?
When you are composing your message, you can arrange for a copy, or blind copy (that is a copy sent to another person without the **To:** recipient's knowledge) to be sent as many people as you wish. This is best done at the time of addressing the email, but it can be done at any time prior to sending.

At the time of addressing
1. Open a new message window, and click the addresses button on the toolbar.

2. Select a recipient from the appropriate address book. At this point you can determine if this person is the main recipient, meant to receive a copy or blind copy. After selecting the contact, press 'To:', 'Cc:', or 'Bcc:' as appropriate (circled in figure 5.44).

Figure 5.44. Setting up Cc and Bcc recipients.

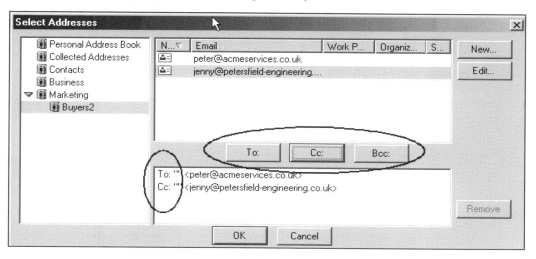

3. After completing the addressing process, click the OK button. The message will now be addressed. Note that in figure 5.45, each recipient's status is indicated in the address box (circled). The message is ready to complete.

Composing and sending emails ....

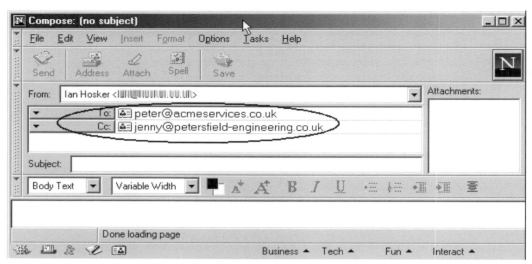

Figure 5.45. The message header shows who are the main recipients, and who will receive copies of the message.

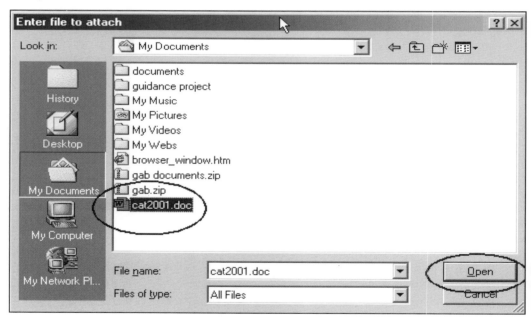

Figure 5.46. Searching for a file to attach to the message.

During composition

It is not unusual to forget to include a recipient and have a minor panic while writing your email message. All is not lost because you can modify the recipient list. Click on the Address button on the toolbar to open the Select Addressees window. You can add, change and remove addressees using the methods described earlier before clicking OK to accept the changes.

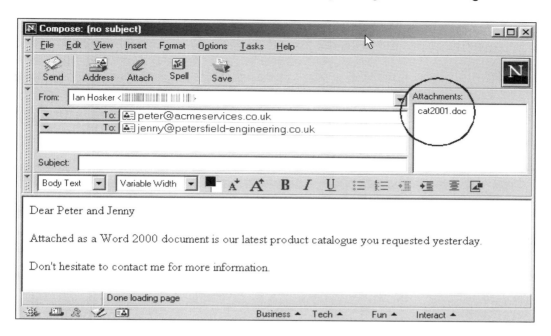

Figure 5.47. Attached files are listed on the right-hand side of the message header.

Attaching files to emails

Attaching files to a Netscape Messenger email message is pretty straightforward. The general method applies to all email software packages. It is best to attach any files before you become too heavily involved in writing the message. You are less likely to forget the attachment.

1. Compose a message in the usual way. Click the Attach button on the toolbar. This will open the 'Enter file to attach' box (figure 5.46). Search for the file you want to attach, select it and click the Open button.

2. On the right hand side of the header there is a box labelled Attachments. You will see the attached file listed (circled in figure 5.47). If you want to attach more than one file, repeat the process for each file. All the attached files will be listed. When you send the message, a copy of the attached files will be sent with it.

Deleting old messages

If you want to get rid of old email you have sent, or are cluttering up your Inbox, just highlight the message and press the Delete button on your keyboard.

Deleted material is sent to the Trash folder. This acts like the Recycle Bin on your Windows Desktop. It gives you the chance to say 'oops!' and recover the file. To delete it from your computer altogether, you must highlight the Trash Folder to reveal its contents and delete the messages from there. You will pass the point of no return when you do this.

Composing and sending emails ....

Tutorial

In this tutorial, you are going to compose and send emails to people you know. You will also ask them to reply to you, and their replies will form the basis of the Tutorial for chapter 6. Their replies will also be confirmation that they have received your messages. Before you begin, though, you should make sure that your computer has an up to date version of an anti-virus program. You may also find it worthwhile installing a firewall program as well to protect your system (see chapters 1 and 4).

▶ *Tip* – Before you begin this tutorial, contact people you know who have internet access and who are competent email users. Discuss the requirements of this tutorial with them and secure their agreement to help you. You are asking them to:

1. support your learning and skill development

2. … by receiving and responding to sample emails.

Exercise 1: Your address book
Create new entries in your email program's address book. There are a couple of things you need to take care over when doing this. You must be 100 per cent accurate when typing email addresses into the address book entry. The internet can be a pretty unforgiving beast and will not deliver email with addresses that are not spot on. If any of your messages are rejected because they are deemed 'undeliverable', a message will be sent back to you (as an email from your ISP's server) telling you of this fact.

▶ *The moral of this* – Double-check as you enter information into your address book. It is so easy to make what appears to be a minor mistake, which makes it impossible to send anything to that person or organisation. The frustrating part about this is that it is sometimes difficult to see the wood from the trees. The mistake is so minor you cannot see it!

Now that you have begun to develop a personalised address book, you can add and delete contacts over time. In chapter 6, you will be shown how to store the contact details of people who send emails to you.

Exercise 2: Sending an email with attachment
Once you have entered the contact details of those friendly types who have kindly consented to being guinea pigs, you can get down to some serious emailing. In this exercise, you are going to generate an email to send to them. The email will therefore have multiple recipients, and will involve the use of an attached file.

First of all, a brief word about the attached file. The easiest way is to create a simple text file, so everyone you email can open and read. Use WordPad or Notepad, the basic word-processing programs included in Windows. Click the **Start** button on the Taskbar, and then **Accessories**. Both programs are usually listed in the Accessories menu.

1. Write a brief message and save it as a text file (will have the TXT suffix – e.g. message.txt) in the **My Documents** folder or somewhere else you can easily remember.

2. Compose an email and address it to everyone in the group who have agreed to help you, asking them to respond to your message to confirm it has been received, complete with the attachment. Include the following paragraph in your message: Thanks for taking part in this exercise. Please reply to this email and return the attached file as an attachment to your reply.

3. Attach the text file and send it.

4. Wait for everyone to respond. The tutorial in chapter 6 will pick up where this exercise left off.

Your learning outcomes checklist

At the beginning of the chapter you were given a list of things you should know or be able to do by the time you had worked through the chapter. These learning outcomes are listed again for you to consider. Use the checklist as a self-assessment tool to see if you can confidently say you have achieved them. Where you feel that you have not achieved a learning outcome, or would like to have another go to make sure, you are given a pointer to the section to revisit.

Outcome	Achieved	If not, or want to recap, revisit
Be able to set up and maintain an address book for use with your email program.		How do I set up an address book?
Be able to compose one or more emails properly addressed.		How do I compose an email? Can I send a copy to someone else?
Be able to create and save emails in draft form.		Can I save a draft of my email while I think about it?
Be able to attach files to an email.		How do I attach files?
Be able to send emails via a dial-up connection.		How do I send my emails?
Be able to delete old email messages.		How do I delete old messages I no longer want to keep?

6 Receiving and responding to email

In this chapter, we will explore:

▶ *learning outcomes for this chapter*
▶ *key points about email*
▶ *Microsoft Outlook and Outlook Express*
▶ *Netscape Messenger*
▶ *tutorial*
▶ *your learning outcomes checklist*

Learning outcomes for this chapter

How to receive and respond to emails from other people is the other part of the story of this form of electronic communication. This chapter looks at how to do this with Microsoft's Outlook and Outlook Express, and with Netscape's Messenger. By the end of the chapter you should be able to:

1. Receive and read email messages sent to you.

2. Reply to email sent to you.

3. Add the sender's details to your address book.

4. Forward a copy of an email to someone else.

5. Save and open attached files.

6. Check attachments for viruses.

Key points about email

'Did you get my message?'
One of the minor irritations in life is of not knowing whether someone has received the email message you sent yesterday. When you send out a letter you expect a delay in receiving a reply, but email is so instantaneous that an immediate response is expected. This is, perhaps, an unreasonable expectation. After all, recipients may not be in the office every day, and may not check their email as often as they should.

Email communications systems are now very reliable, but messages can still go astray. If you receive a message that you do not consider to be junk, it is good etiquette to at least acknowledge receipt. This is quick and easy to do. Even if the message requires a more considered response – one that you cannot give immediately

– a quick acknowledgement lets the sender know you have received it. This is an example of good **netiquette**.

Handling files attached to emails
In chapter 5, you were shown how to use email as a method of transferring files to other people, such as a word-processed report. Of course, this can work the other way, and other people can send email attachments to you. This has many obvious advantages in a business setting – sharing reports for example – but you will need to know how to handle these attachments. We will show how to view or save them, and how to check them over for possible viruses.

Coping with the threat of viruses
An email message in itself is unlikely to infect your computer with a virus. A virus is far more likely to be associated with an attached file. That file may be infected by a virus itself, or it may be a virus program in its own right.

▶ *Caution* – Never open any attached files without scanning them first with an anti-virus program (chapter 4). When in doubt, avoid opening or saving any attachments. Even attachments from trusted sources should be checked for viruses.

Forwarding email messages to other people
Some things are too good to keep to yourself. There will be times when messages contain information you want to share with others. Email programs have the facility to 'forward' a message. In other words, the message can be copied to someone else. In effect, you are emailing the original message, with the chance to add your own message by way of explanation.

Saving email addresses
You may often receive mail from someone whose details are not in your address book. Sometimes the contact will be important enough for you to want a permanent record of it. There is a quick and easy way to add a new email contact to your address book.

Microsoft Outlook and Outlook Express

How do I receive and read emails?
Both Outlook and Outlook Express send and receive emails as part of the same operation. In chapter 5, you were shown how to send emails you have composed. When you go online, the program will go through a two-stage process:

1. Emails which you have composed, and which are waiting in the **Outbox**, will be sent.

2. The program then seeks and receives emails waiting for you on the mail server.

Receiving and responding to email ....

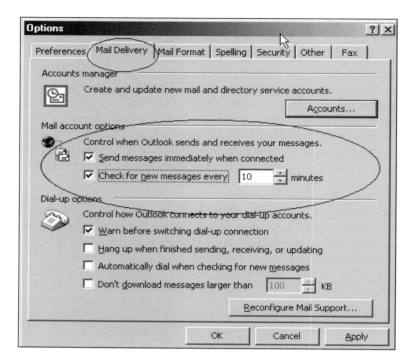

Figure 6.1. The timing of automatic email delivery while online in Outlook

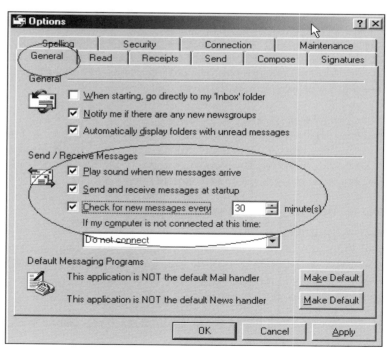

Figure 6.2. The timing of automatic email delivery while online in Outlook Express.

Automatic downloading of messages

If you are permanently online, Outlook and Outlook Express will automatically check for and download messages from your ISP's mail server. You can set the frequency with which Outlook and Outlook express carry out this action.

Select Tools > Options from the menu bar to open the options window. Here, you can configure (adjust) the way your program operates. Figures 6.1 and 6.2 show the option boxes for Outlook and Outlook Express respectively. You can alter the frequency settings by clicking on the appropriate tab and changing the time settings (circled area in both figures).

Manual checking for and downloading of messages

You can use keyboard shortcuts to tell Outlook and Outlook Express to go online to send emails and check for incoming mail. You can use this method if you are operating a dial-up connection rather than being permanently online. You can also use it if you want to check for incoming mail in between the times you have set for automatic checking as described above.

▶ *Outlook* – Press the F5 function key.

▶ *Outlook Express* – Press down the Ctrl and M keys at the same time.

In both cases, if you have a dial-up connection, the dial-up box will open asking you to go online. When you click OK, the computer's modem will dial your ISP and connect to the server when answered. A progress box will appear to show you what is going on in terms of sending and receiving mail (figure 6.3). If you are operating via a com-

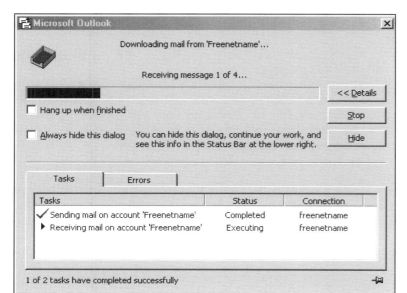

Figure 6.3. The download progress box if you have a dial-up connection.

Receiving and responding to email ....

pany network, you will not see this box. Instead, you will see a small message box indicating that the program is checking for incoming mail.

What if I don't have any email to send?

You can still receive emails even if you have none to send. Using F5 in Outlook, or Ctrl + M in Outlook Express will enable you to go online. In this case, though, the progress box (figure 6.1) will not have the line 'Sending mail on account...' It will simply check to see if there is any mail to receive.

How will the program tell me there is mail to read?

Email received is automatically stored in the program's Inbox. You will see a number in square brackets, coloured blue, next to the Inbox. You will This tells you how many messages have been received (figure 6.4). Actually, it is the number of *unread* emails, which is not quite the same thing. You can receive emails, but may choose not read them right away, so the computer logs them as 'unread' to remind you that mail is still waiting to be read.

Figure 6.4. Outlook (right) and Outlook Express (left) show there is one unread message.

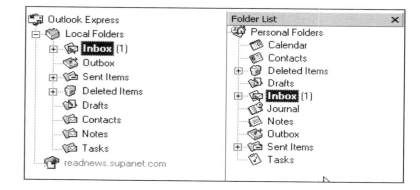

How can I read my email?

1. Click on the Inbox in the folders window. You will see a list of the Inbox contents in the right-hand upper window of Outlook or Outlook Express. This will contain all your mail, including the messages you have previously read. Unread mail is always symbolised by a sealed envelope symbol (circled in figure 6.5). Read mail is symbolised by an open envelope.

2. To read a message, double-click on it in the list to open it. You may need to maximise the window if it is too small to read conveniently. When you have finished reading the message, you can close the window by clicking on the X in the top left-hand corner of the message (figure 6.6). This will take you back to the Inbox view.

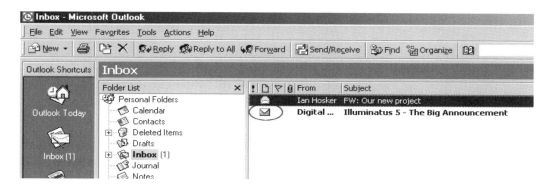

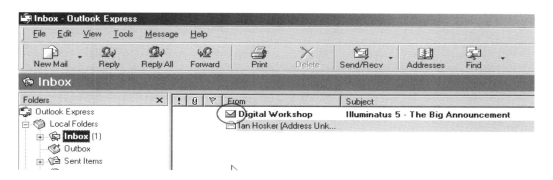

3. You can read other messages in the same way. Notice that the sealed envelope symbols turn into open envelopes once they have been read. You can also re-read old messages by double-clicking on them.

Figure 6.5. The existence of unread mail is shown as little sealed envelopes.

4. If you want to delete a message, simply highlight it in the list by clicking on it once. Then click the Delete button on the toolbar. You can also delete the message while you are reading it. In figure 6.6, the delete tool is available in the message toolbar. This allows you to read junk mail you have no reason to keep. That action alone will help to keep your Inbox free of huge lists of old redundant mail.

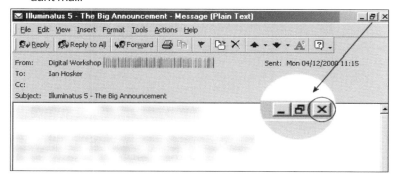

Figure 6.6. You can close a message window by clicking on the X.

Receiving and responding to email ....

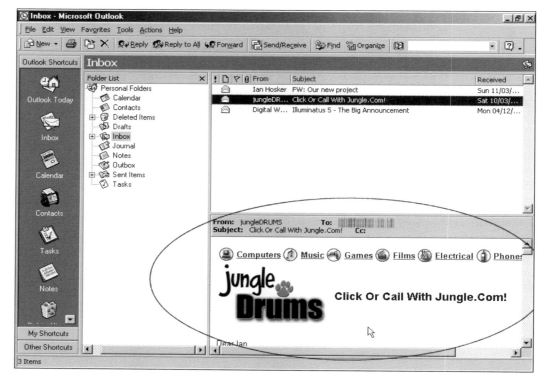

Figure 6.7. The preview window in Outlook. Outlook Express has a similar window.

Can I preview my mail?

The bottom right-hand window previews the message currently highlighted in the mail list (upper right-hand window). This is a good way of prioritising mail. Click once on a message in the list and its content will be shown in the preview window (figure 6.7). You can trawl through message to message in the list, and even delete those you do not want to bother with (e.g. unsolicited and unwanted email).

How do I reply to email?

If you want to reply to email, there are two buttons on the toolbar (figure 6.8) that will let you do this quickly and easily:

▶ *Reply* – Use this button if you want to reply to the sender only.

▶ *Reply to All* – This will ensure that your reply is sent to everyone listed in the 'To:' and 'Cc:' boxes which is useful if the message is part of a consultation or conferencing activity and ensures that

Figure 6.8. The reply buttons in Outlook (left) and Outlook Express (right).

Outlook

Outlook Express

everyone involved gets all the information.

After reading a message, and deciding you want to reply, click either the Reply or Reply to All button (see above). This will automatically open a new message window already addressed to the recipient(s)

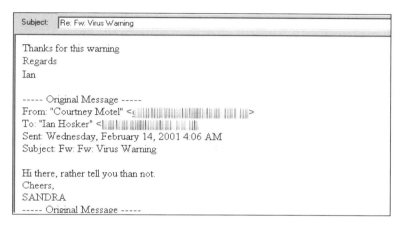

Figure 6.9. The reply to a message will also carry a copy of the original message.

(see figure 6.9). If the original message contained an attached file, this will not be copied.

You will also notice that the new message window contains a copy of the original message (including the header details). This way, when you reply, the original sender will know the context of the reply. The text cursor will be placed above this and you should type in your reply there. When you are ready, click the Send button.

How do I add the sender's details to my address book?
Adding the email address of a new contact to your address book could not be easier. If you receive an email message from a new contact, you can capture their details using the right-hand mouse button! You can also use this method to add the contact details of other recipients of the message.

1. The header of the message will contain the name of the sender and other recipients. Click once on the name you want to add to

 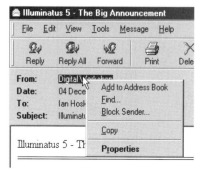

Figure 6.10. Right clicking the mouse over the sender's name opens a sub-menu in Outlook (left) and Outlook Express (right). You can add the sender's name to your address book this way.

107

Receiving and responding to email ....

highlight it. While still pointing at the name, click the right-hand mouse button and an action menu will appear (figure 6.10).

2. One of the options in the action menu will be Add to Contacts, Add to Address Book or Add to Personal Address Book. The particular option will depend on how your system has been set up. For example, in a company network, a general address book may be available to everyone, while individuals are enabled to set up a Personal Address Book of their own.

3. If you are operating from home or a single computer, the address book will be called **Contacts** in Outlook, or **Address Book** in Outlook Express. Select the option available to you. This will open a new address book entry window (as described in chapter 5) for you to edit or add any additional information about this contact (see figure 6.11).

Figure 6.11. Outlook (left) and Outlook Express (right).

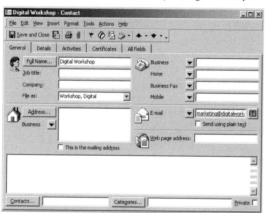
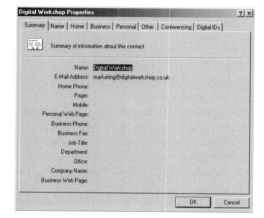

Figure 6.12. The message forwarding buttons in Outlook (left) and Outlook Express (right).

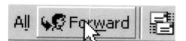

Figure 6.13. Forwarding a message will also forward any attachments. Outlook (left) and Outlook Express (right).

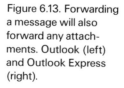

4. Click the 'Save and Close' button (Outlook) or OK button (Outlook Express) on the contacts window toolbar when you have captured all the information you need. This contact will now be recorded in your address book for future reference.

Can I forward email to a friend or colleague?

1. If you decide that the message you are reading is too good to keep to yourself, you can forward a copy to one or more other people. Click the Forward button on the message's toolbar (figure 6.12).

2. This action will open a new message window with the original message copied, including header details. The new message will not be addressed to anyone. You will therefore need to type in the email addresses in the 'To:', 'Cc:' and 'Bcc': boxes, or call them up from your address book. If there are any attached files, the new forwarding message will also have a copy of them attached (figure 6.13). You can type in your message above the message you are forwarding before clicking the Send button.

How do I save and open attached files?

When you look inside the Inbox, messages with attached files will be listed with a small paperclip next to them (circled in figure 6.14).

How to identify attached files

1. Click on the message whose attachments you want to identify. The preview window will show a paperclip symbol (circled in figure 6.15).

2. Click on the paperclip. This will bring up a list of the attached files so that you can identify them. The list will provide the full name of the file including its file extension (figure 6.16). This will help you decide on the authenticity of the file, i.e. can it be trusted?

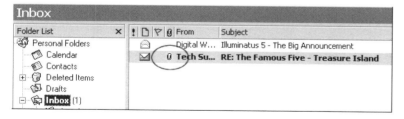

Figure 6.14. Messages carrying attached files are identified by the paperclip symbol.

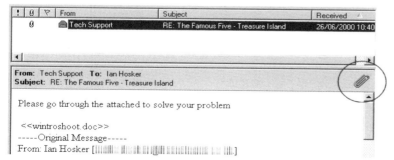

Figure 6.15. The paperclip symbol in the preview window indicates attached files.

Figure 6.16. Clicking on the paperclip produces a list of the attached files.

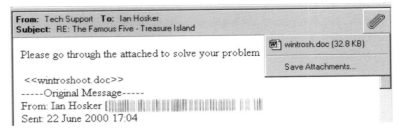

How to open an attached file

There are two ways of opening attached files in Outlook and Outlook Express. In figure 6.16, you can view the name of the file or files (and also their size in memory terms). If you now click on the file name, it automatically opens it. This assumes that your computer has the correct application installed.

You can also open the attachment while you are viewing the email message. Here, there is a slight difference between Outlook and Outlook Express.

Figure 6.17. Outlook. Double-clicking on the icon will open the file.

▶ *Outlook* – The attachment is shown as an icon at the bottom of the message window (figure 6.17). Double click on the icon to open the attachment.

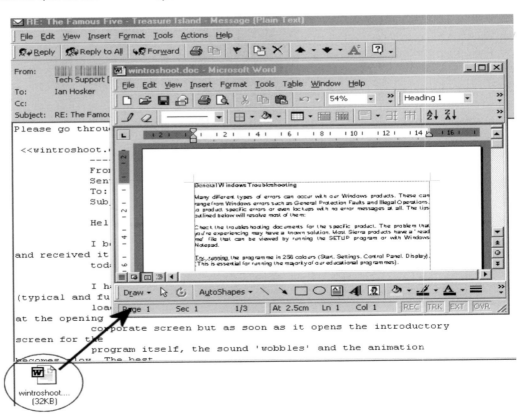

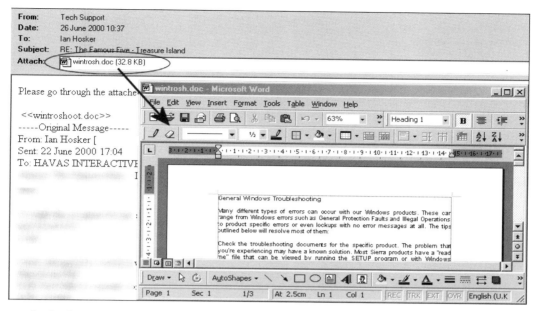

▶ *Outlook Express* – Attachments are listed in the message header (figure 6.18). Double-clicking on the name of an attachment will open it.

Figure 6.18. Outlook Express. Double-clicking on the name of the attached file listed in the header will open it.

Saving attached files in Outlook

The methods of saving attachments in Outlook and Outlook Express are similar, with just a minor difference in the look of the windows.

In Outlook, select File, Save Attachments from the menu bar. A box will open with the attachments listed. By default they are all highlighted, as it is assumed that you will want to save all the attachments (figure 6.19). Click OK. This will open a Save window (figure 6.20) where you select where you want the attachments saved to. Click OK to save the files.

Figure 6.19. Saving attachments while viewing the message in Outlook or Outlook Express.

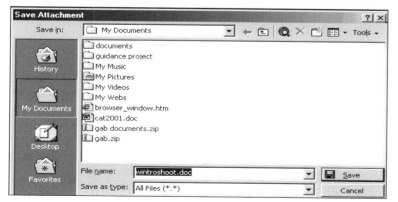

Figure 6.20. Outlook. Save the file in a suitable location. You can also change the name if you wish.

Receiving and responding to email ....

Figure 6.21. Outlook
Express. Use the Browse
button to find a suitable
location for saving the
attachment.

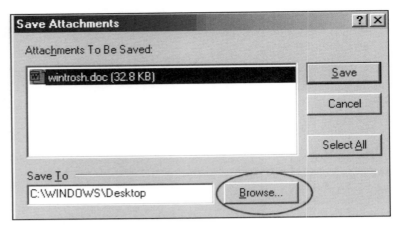

Saving attached files in Outlook Express
Select File, Save Attachments from the menu bar. The window that
now opens is slightly different to that in Outlook. The attached files
are listed, and you are asked to identify the location where they
should be saved. A default location is listed in the Save to box
(figure 6.21), but you can click the Browse button to look for another,
more convenient location.

How can I check that incoming mail is virus-free?
This method assumes that when you point to a file and click the right-
hand mouse button, there is an option in the action menu list to scan
the files with your anti-virus program. If this option is not available,
you will have to open the anti-virus program and scan the file from
there. If you do find a virus in an attached file, you must delete it as
described below. You must also do two other things:

(a) Scan your hard drive for viruses and clean out any that are found.

(b) Email the person who sent you the 'infected' attachment and let
them know of the problem – they may be totally unaware of the
problem so its gives them the chance to 'clean' their computer
and, with luck, trace the source. In
this way, it is theoretically possible to
trace the infection route back to its
source.

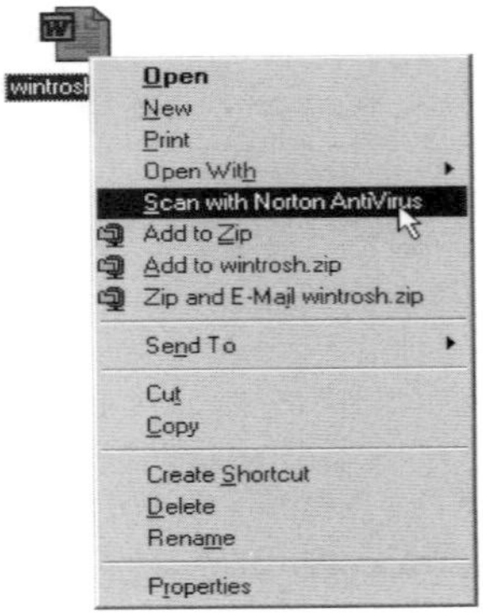

Figure 6.22. Right-click
on the file to open the
action menu. Select scan
with the anti-virus
program.

If you initially save attached files to your
computer's Desktop, it will be a simple
matter to scan them. You won't need to
browse your way to some location deep
inside your computer's folder system.
Point to the downloaded file and click
the right-hand mouse button. This will
open the action menu (figure 6.22).

▶ *Caution* – Do not double-click with the left-hand mouse button. This will open the file and may activate a virus that is lurking there.

Select the option to scan the file with your anti-virus program. This will activate the scan. What happens next depends on the condition of the file. If the scan does not detect a virus, you will see a message telling you so (figure 6.23).

Figure 6.23. This is the message you want to see after a scan!

Repair or delete the infected file?
If the scan does detect a virus, or suspect code within the file that suggests the possible presence of a virus, the program will tell you this. It should also provide options as what to do with the file, such as to repair or delete it. You can certainly opt to repair the file, but there is still a risk. It is much safer to delete the file and inform the sender that they have transmitted a virus.

Deleting a file manually
To delete a file manually, point to it and click the right-hand mouse button to open the action menu. Select Delete. This will transfer the file to the Recycle Bin on your Desktop screen. To remove it from your computer completely, point to the Recycle Bin and click the right-hand mouse button to open another action menu.

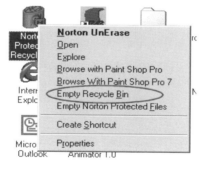

Figure 6.24. Delete suspect files from your computer without delay!

Select Empty Recycle Bin (figure 6.24). You will get a message asking if you are sure. Click Yes, because you will never be surer about deleting anything from your computer!

Netscape Messenger

How do I receive and read emails?
You can configure Messenger to automatically check for and download messages at prescribed intervals. Or, you can manually check and download messages any time between these set times.

Automatic downloading of messages
Use the following method to set the frequency with which to check for and download messages. This method is designed for when the program is permanently online.

1. From the menu bar select Edit, Mail/News Account Settings. This will open the Account Settings box showing your account details.

Receiving and responding to email ....

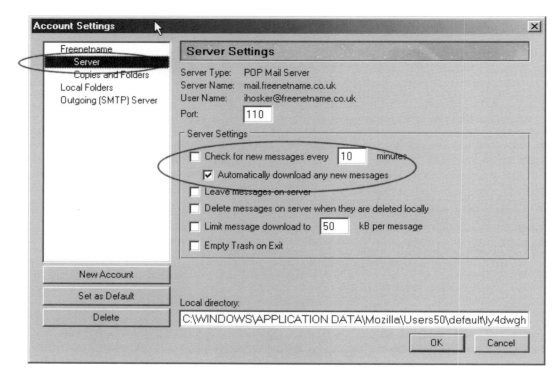

Figure 6.25. Editing the message download settings in Netscape.

2. In the right-hand side of the box (circled in figure 6.25) select Server. This will reveal the server details in the right-hand side of the box. You can set the frequency with which to check for messages (circled in figure 6.25), or tick the check box for Automatically download any new messages. This will download messages as soon as they arrive at your ISP's mail server.

3. Click OK to accept any changes.

Manual checking for and downloading of messages
Netscape has been designed to be permanently online when open. It is awkward to use as an offline program, making it less flexible than Outlook or Outlook Express.

Figure 6.26. The Get Msg button overrides automatic settings and causes the program to check for new messages.

Messenger will receive messages automatically in accordance with the Account Settings described in the previous section, provided you are connected to the internet. If you want to override these settings and check for mail, simply press the Get Msg button on the toolbar (circled in figure 6.26).

Figure 6.27. You may need to type in the password for the account you have logged on with.

Before the program connects you to the server, you may be asked for your password for the email account. Type in your password and click OK (figure 6.27).

If there is any mail waiting for you, it will be downloaded into your Inbox. You will know that you have new mail, because the Inbox will display the number of new messages in brackets and the listed messages will be in bold (figure 6.28).

Figure 6.28. New messages will be stored in the Inbox. The number in brackets is the number of unread messages.

How can I read my email in Messenger?

Click on the Inbox in the folders window. A list of its contents can be viewed in the upper right-hand window (figure 6.29). To read a message, simply double click on it with the left-hand mouse button. This will open the message-viewing window. When you have finished reading the message, close the viewing window by clicking the X in the top right-hand corner of the window.

Figure 6.29. After viewing a message, close the message window by clicking on the X.

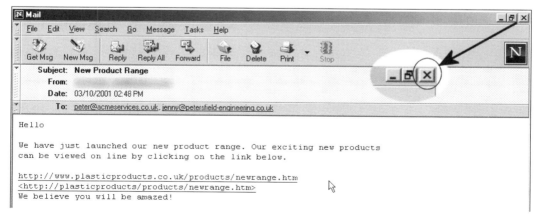

Receiving and responding to email ....

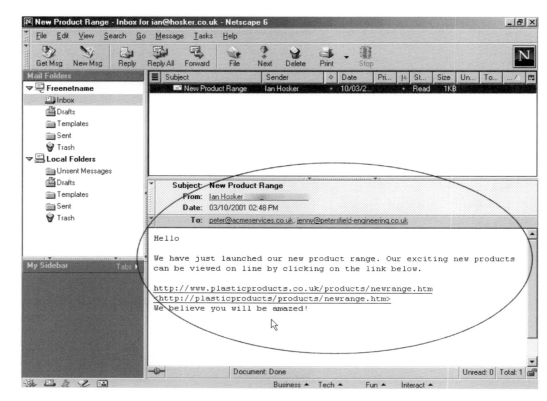

Figure 6.30. The preview window (circled) enables you to view part of a message's contents before you open the message.

Can I preview my mail?
The bottom right-hand window provides a preview of your mail. Simply clicking once on a message in the top window will produce its preview below (figure 6.30). This is a useful way of quickly scanning a lot of incoming mail so you can prioritise the various messages.

How do I reply to email in Messenger?
As you read a message, you may decide to reply. There are two buttons on the toolbar that enable you to do this easily (figure 6.31).

▶ *Reply* – This button lets you set up a reply to the sender.

▶ *ReplyAll* – This button will set up a reply to the sender and all recipients of the message, a useful facility in email conferencing.

Figure 6.31. The reply buttons on the message window tool bar.

To set up a reply to the message you are reading, click the Reply or Reply All button, as appropriate. This will open up a new message already addressed to the sender (and other recipient if you used the Reply All button) (figure 6.32). Note that the Reply window carries a copy of the original message, but not a copy of

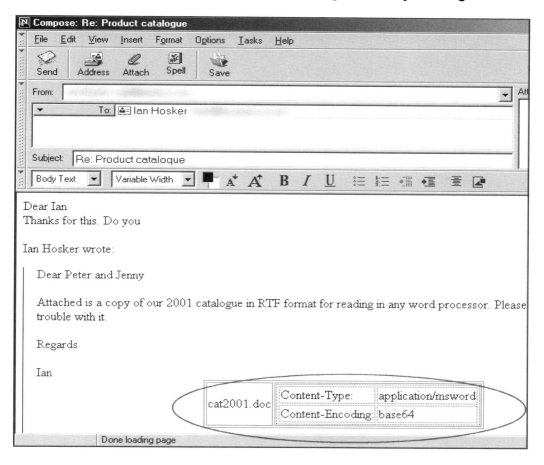

Figure 6.32. The reply message window contains the full text of, and a list of any files attached to, the original message.

any attached files. However, the message does show that the original message carried an attachment (circled in figure 6.32)

You can type your reply and send the message. This is just like composing a normal message, so now you can attach a file if you want.

Can I add the sender to my Messenger address book?

You can add the address of a sender or other recipients listed in the message header to your address book quite easily. You can do this either from the preview pane, or while reading the message in full.

Point to the name you want to add and click the right-hand mouse button. A short action menu with two options will open (figure 6.33). The second option (Send Mail To) lets you send a message to the highlighted contact and will open a new message window addressed to the contact. Select 'Add Address to Address Book'.

A New Card box will open with the basic information added (figure 6.34). If you have more contact details, you can add them to the address book record card before clicking OK. The new contact's details will be added to your address book.

Receiving and responding to email ....

Figure 6.33. Adding a sender's details as a new contact to your address book.

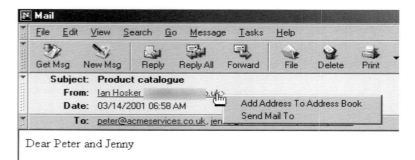

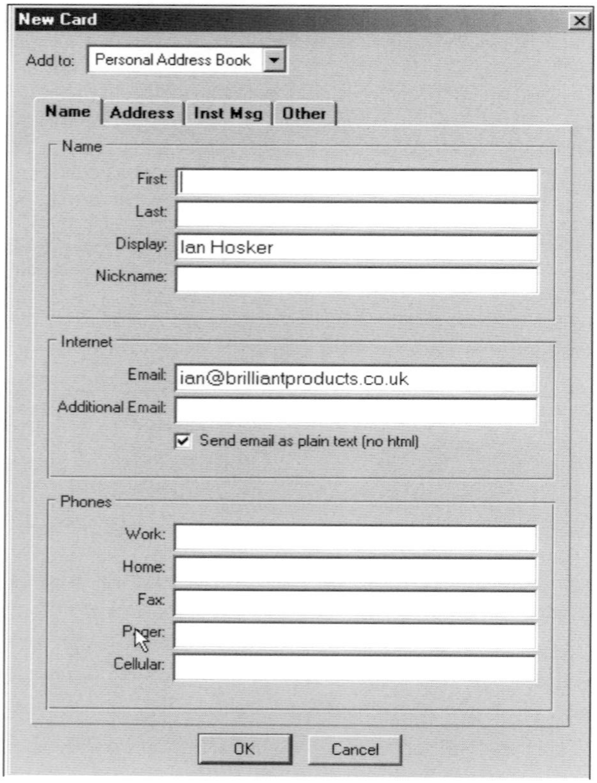

Figure 6.34. The basic details of your new contact are already added to the Address Book card.

Can I forward email to a friend or colleague?
Using Messenger, a copy of a message you are reading can be forwarded to one or more other people. Click the Forward button on the message's toolbar (figure 6.35). This will open a new message window with the original message copied, including header details.

Figure 6.35. The forwarding button on the message window tool bar.

The new message will not be addressed to anyone so you will need to type in the email addresses in the 'To:' ,'Cc:' and 'Bcc:' boxes, or call them up from your address book. Any attached files in the original message will be forwarded, too (figure 6.36).

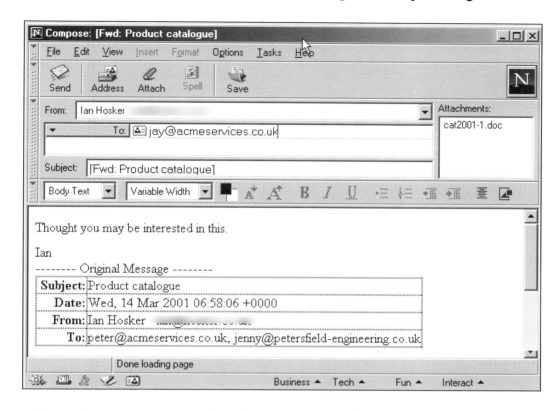

You can type in your message above the message you are forwarding. When you are ready, you can send the message or store it for sending later.

Figure 6.36. The forwarded message window contains the text of the original message. Files attached to the original message are also forwarded.

How do I save and open attached files in Messenger?

The list of messages will not indicate whether or not there are any attachments. However, if you select the message, the preview window will show a paperclip icon in the top right-hand corner of the window, and the number of attached files (circled in figure 6.37). The same icon is present when the message is viewed in full.

You can do this in the preview window or while you are reading the message. Click on the paperclip icon in the corner (circled in figure 6.37) to display a list of the attachments, using their file names and extensions.

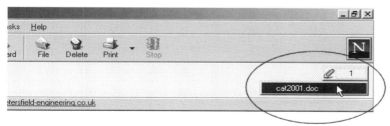

Figure 6.37. Open a list of attached files by clicking on the paperclip symbol in the preview or message window.

RTF format for reading in any word processor. Please let me know if you have

Receiving and responding to email ....

Figure 6.38. Clicking on a listed message opens a decision-making box: save or open the file?

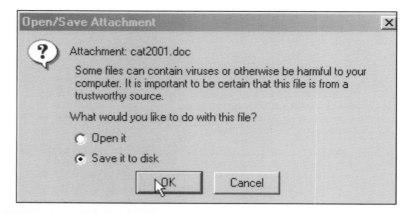

Figure 6.39. If you elect to save the file, you will be asked to specify a location for saving the file.

If you click on a file name, a dialog box will open asking if you want to open the file or save it to disk (figure 6.38). The default setting is 'Save it to disk'. Accepting this option results in a Save Attachment box (figure 6.39) where you can, for example, state the location where you would like to save the file.

You can, of course choose to open the file rather than save it. In this case, select Open in the dialog box (figure 6.38). After clicking OK, Messenger will try to open it but will first present you with a dialog box to confirm or identify the program to be used (figure 6.40).

Messenger prefers you to save attached files rather than open them directly, a more long-winded operation than with Outlook or Outlook Express. However, saving a file first is far preferable to opening it directly. This is because of the risk of viruses. If you open a file without first checking that it is clean, your whole system is at risk.

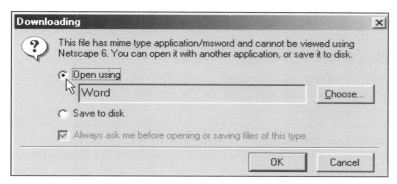

Figure 6.40. If you elect to open a file, you may be asked to specify the program to use.

Can I check that incoming mail is not carrying a virus?
The approach to this was described earlier in the chapter in relation to Outlook and Outlook Express (page 112-113). The same approach applies to Netscape Messenger.

Tutorial

By now, the 'volunteers' to whom you sent messages as part of the chapter 5 tutorial should have responded. Each person should have sent an acknowledgement of having received your message. They should also have attached the text file and returned it to you (necessary for this chapter's tutorial).

1. Go online with your email software and check for the replies you are expecting. If you have not received any (or not from everyone), compose and send a message to gently remind them. Check your mail again in a day or so.

2. Acknowledge the mail you have received. Tip: you can write one message and address it to all those who have responded, rather than write several separate messages.

3. Save the attachment from one of the messages. (It is difficult to save more than one copy unless you save them in different areas of your computer because they will all have the same name – alternatively, you could save them using different names.)

4. Scan your saved attachment with your anti-virus program. This is quite important because even though it is the same file you sent out in the last tutorial, it is possible for a virus to have been picked up from the recipient's machine.

5. For the purpose of this exercise, assume your file has a virus. Delete it from your computer (do not forget to empty the Recycle Bin!). If your program has detected a virus, delete it without delay. You should also email the sender and tell them that they have transmitted a virus to you. They may be quite unaware of the virus

Receiving and responding to email ....

lurking on their machine, so will appreciate your message. Of course, don't do that at this point unless there really *was* a virus!

Your learning outcomes checklist

At the beginning of the chapter you were given a list of things you should know, or be able to do, by the time you had worked through the chapter. These learning outcomes are listed again for you to consider. Use the checklist as a self-assessment tool to see if you can confidently say you have achieved them.

Where you feel that you have not achieved a learning outcome, or would like to have another go to make sure, you are given a pointer to the section to revisit.

Outcome	Achieved	If not, or want to recap, revisit
To receive and read email messages sent to you.		How do I receive and read emails?
To reply to email sent to you.		How do I reply to email?
To add the sender's details to your address book.		Can I add the sender's details to my address book?
To forward a copy of an email to someone else.		Can I forward email to a friend or colleague?
To save and open attached files.		How do I save and open attached files?
To check attachments for viruses.		Can I check that incoming mail is not carrying a virus?

7 A practical scenario

In this chapter, we will explore:

▶ *using the internet as a business research tool*
▶ *doing the research*
▶ *creating and emailing the report*

. . . .

The purpose of this chapter is to bring together the knowledge and skills developed in the earlier chapters. We will use a realistic scenario set inside an organisation. The project is designed to help you develop your research and communication skills using the internet.

This scenario is meant to be interactive. In other words, you will be asked to respond to real email messages, and to communicate directly with the author of this book (Ian Hosker) as part of the process. Be ready to send and receive emails with your email address. The aim is to give you an opportunity to practise your skills and knowledge – for real!

Stage 1: Using the internet as a business research tool

Context

You are a marketing assistant working for a company that specialises in compiling market reports for a range of clients. One of your clients has sent you the following email message.

From: Ian Hosker [ianhosker@yahoo.com]
Subject: Market Analysis

Hello J

Our company is looking at how we can market our new product range in Australia and the United States. We think we would like to concentrate our initial efforts on market testing in, say, New South Wales and California.

Can you put together a report telling us who may be useful whole-sale (or retail) outlets for the new range? We want to know who they are, with some basic background information, including which to contact (with their e-mail addresses if possible) and company web site addresses. As usual, we want it last week!! Let us know when you could supply the report. I assume the usual fee applies?
Regards

Ian

There are a couple of problems with this message, in that important pieces of information are missing. Let's be kind and say the sender has done this in a hurry. He knows what he wants, but has rushed the message out and forgotten to brief you on two key points:

1. What exactly is this new product range?

2. What is the market his company is aiming for?

Task 1
Respond to the email message, acknowledging receipt and seeking clarification of the two points listed above.

Stage 2: Doing the research

Context
There are many ways of gathering market information about another country. Most embassies and High Commissions collate basic information as part of their function to promote trade between their country and that in which they are based. However, for the purpose of this exercise, you will use the internet as your research tool.

The outcome of successfully completing Task 1 will be an email from the author giving you more specific information about the market research you need to do. The return message will have contained the following information:

1. The product range that will be market tested.

2. The key markets the company wants to target for the products.

You will also have been given additional instructions.

Task 2
Carry out your internet research in accordance with your new instructions to gather information meeting the client's needs. The key skills here are:

1. Ability to use basic and advanced searches.

2. Ability to select a search engine most likely to yield the best results.

3. Ability to store, print and read web pages offline.

4. Ability to identify web pages and sites that are a close match to your client's requirements.

Remember to allow yourself plenty of time for this task, so you can do a reasonable job of searching for appropriate sites.

Stage 3: Creating and emailing the report

Context

The internet research stage will have taught you the value of being well organised and highly selective! All the pages you have visited will be cached – that is a copy stored in the History folder. You may have opted to print pages or cache them deliberately so you do not have to spend too much time on the internet.

Here you visit a page and let it load completely, then hit the back button (to return to the search results list) and visit another site. When you have finished, go offline and use the History facility to view and evaluate the value of pages at leisure.

Task 3

1. You now need to identify the companies that your client is likely to find useful to approach to market test the new product range. Create a short word-processed report (say two sides of A4) listing the good contacts – web site address, and any contact email addresses.

2. Email the report to your client as an attached file to the message. Do not forget to add a covering note in the body of the email message.

And finally...

To return to the main reason behind the publication of this book, the ability to use the internet in the workplace is becoming more highly valued by employers. Of course, being able to use the web, and being able to make productive use of it, can be two quite different things! Using the internet only occasionally will not lose you the skill, but you do need to use it regularly to develop good 'local knowledge'. For example, after a while you will get to know which are the best search engines for your work needs and the best way to structure keyword criteria. And if you can use the internet productively at work, you will also be able to use it more productively at play!

Appendix: Qualifications in internet skills

Awarding bodies

There is a growing number of courses and qualifications in the use of the internet. The two main awarding bodies, which most employers will recognise as having standing in terms of providing people with work relevant skills and knowledge, are OCR (formerly called the RSA) and City and Guilds. Their web sites and relevant qualifications are given below.

City and Guilds

Welcome to
City & Guilds

- City & Guilds
- City & Guilds International
- Nebs Management
- Pitman Qualifications
- Walled Garden

City and Guilds of London Institute
Customer Services Enquiry Unit
1 Giltspur Street
London EC1A 9DD

Web address: www.city-and-guilds.co.uk
Email address: enquiry@city-and-guilds.co.uk

Qualifications
City and Guilds has a modular qualification called the 7261 series. The modules cover a very wide range of IT applications and technical IT subjects, at three levels – allowing you to progress. A number of the modules cover email, web browsing and web page design.

OCR

Web address: www.ocr.org.uk
Email address: cib@ocr.org.uk
Telephone: 024 76 470033

OCR stands for Oxford, Cambridge and RSA (Royal Society of Arts). It is a fairly new examining body formed by UCLES (the University of Cambridge Local Examinations Syndicate) and the RSA Examinations Board. Its purpose is to develop, promote and provide a flexible range of qualifications which recognise the achievements of learners through all the phases of life and work. The home page offers links into the background of OCR, a news desk, examination officer support, qualifications and a search facility. The qualification link leads to information about GCSEs, AS levels, A levels, key skills, GNVQs and vocational qualifications. Among its most popular awards is CLAIT (computer literacy and information technology), which attracts around 380,000 candidates a year. Over two million people in the UK now hold CLAIT certificates.

Internet Technologies Stage 1
This course covers the basic skills of email, web browsing and web page design.

Internet Technologies Stage 2
This course teaches how to create a web site that would be suitable for a small business not wanting to go to the expense of using professional web site design companies.

BBC Webwise

This ten-hour course has been developed by the BBC out of its very successful series of one-hour taster sessions run through a network of centres throughout the UK. The course has now been incorporated in the OCR entry-level qualification in IT-CLAIT (Computer Literacy and Information Technology) as a separate module.

Where can I join a course?

Most community and adult education centres today offer courses in IT, including internet training. Their addresses will be found in your local library and in yellow pages.

Learndirect
www.learndirect.co.uk
Alternatively, you could call Learndirect on 0800 100 900. This body was set up by the UK Department for Education and Skills (DfES). It is a free information and advice service to help people find local learning opportunities. They will put you in touch with a local provider. With Learndirect courses, you can learn over the internet, at home, at work, at a local centre, whatever suits you best. On its web site you can search through a database of around 800 courses to find one that suits you. Some courses only take about 15 minutes to complete, others up to several hours. Most are available online. Some use workbooks, CD ROMs and videos which you will receive you once you have enrolled.

How much do these courses cost?
Sometimes a short introductory course will be free. Longer courses leading to a qualification will be charged, but certain categories of learners may find that it is free or that there are substantial concessions on fees.

Individual Learning Accounts
www.my-ila.com
If you do have to pay, you may be eligible for a government subsidy in the form of an Individual Learning Account (ILA). These were introduced to encourage as many people as possible to take up learning

opportunities. At the time of writing, an ILA will give you a subsidy of 80 per cent of the cost of some IT courses (up to a maximum of £200 in any one year), and 20 per cent off other courses (up to a maximum of £100 in any one year). For more information call the Individual Learning Account Centre on 0800 072 5678.

Glossary of internet terms

access provider – The company that provides you with access to the internet.

ActiveX – A Microsoft programming language that allows effects such as animations, games and other interactive features to be included a web page.

Adobe Acrobat – A type of software required for reading PDF files ('portable document format'). You may need to have Adobe Acrobat Reader when downloading large text files from the internet, such as lengthy reports or chapters from books.

address book – A directory in a web browser where you can store people's email addresses. This saves having to type them out each time you want to email someone. You just click on an address whenever you want it.

ADSL – Asymmetric Digital Subscriber Line. It is a new phone line technology developed by British Telecommunications in the UK to provide an internet connection speed several times faster than a typical modem.

AltaVista – One of the half dozen most popular internet search engines. Just type in a few key words to find what you want on the internet. See: www.altavista.com

AOL – America OnLine, the world's biggest internet service provider, with more than 27 million subscribers, and now merged with Time Warner.

Apple Macintosh – A type of computer that has its own proprietary operating system, as distinct from the MSDOS and Windows operating systems found on PCs (personal computers).

applet – An application programmed in Java that is designed to run on a web browser. See also **Java**.

application – Any program, such as a word processor or spreadsheet program, designed for use on your computer.

ASCII – American Standard Code for Information Interchange. It is a simple text file format that can be accessed by most word processors and text editors. It is a universal file type for passing textual information across the internet.

Ask Jeeves – A popular internet search engine: www.askjeeves.co.uk

attachment – A file sent with an email message. The attached file can be anything from a word-processed document to a database, spreadsheet, graphic, or even a sound or video file. For example you could email someone birthday greetings, and attach a sound track or video clip.

backup – A second copy of a file or a set of files. Backing up data is essential if there is any risk of data loss.

bandwidth – The width of the electronic highway that gives you access to the internet. The higher the bandwidth, the wider this highway, and the faster the traffic can flow.

banner ad – This is a band of text and graphics, usually situated at the top of a web page. It acts like a title, telling the user what the content of the page is about. It invites the visitor to click on it to visit that site. Banner advertising has become big business.

baud rate – The data transmission speed in a modem, measured in kps (kilobits per second).

BBS – Bulletin board service. A facility to read and to post public messages on a particular web site.

binary numbers – The numbering system used by computers. It only uses 1s and 0s to represent numbers.

Blue Ribbon Campaign – A widely supported campaign for free speech on the internet. See the Electronic Frontier Foundation at: www.eff.org

bookmark – A file of URLs of your favourite internet sites. In the Internet Explorer browser and AOL they are called Favorites.

Glossary of internet terms ....

bot – Short for robot. It is used to refer to a program that will perform a task on the internet, such as carrying out a search.

browser – Your browser is your window to the internet, and will normally supplied by your internet service provider when you first sign up. It is the program that you use to access the world wide web, and manage your personal communications and privacy when online. By far the two most popular browsers are Netscape Communicator and its dominant rival Microsoft Internet Explorer. America Online has its own proprietary browser which is not available separately.

bug – A weakness in a program or a computer system.

bulletin board – A type of computer-based news service that provides an email service and a file archive.

cache – A file storage area on a computer. Your web browser will normally cache (copy to your hard drive) each web page you visit. When you revisit that page on the web, you may in fact be looking at the page originally cached on your computer. To be sure you are viewing the current page, press Reload or Refresh on your browser toolbar.

certificate – A computer file that securely identifies a person or organisation on the internet.

channel (chat) – Place where you can chat with other internet chatters. The name of a chat channel is prefixed with a hash mark, #.

click stream – The sequence of hyperlinks clicked by someone when using the internet.

click through This is when someone clicks on a banner ad or other link, for example, and is moved from that page to the advertiser's web site.

client – This is the term given to the program that you use to access the internet. For example your web browser is a web client, and your email program is an email client.

configure – To set up, or adjust the settings, of a computer or software program.

content – The text, articles, images, columns and sales messages of a web site.

cookie – A cookie is a small text code that the server of a web page asks your browser to store on your hard drive. It may be used to store password or registration details, and pass information about your site usage to the web site concerned.

cracker – Someone who breaks into computer systems with the intention of causing some kind of damage or abusing the system in some way.

crash – What happens when a computer program malfunctions. The operating system of your PC may perform incorrectly or come to a complete stop ('freeze'), forcing you to shut down and restart ('reboot').

cyberspace – Popular term for the intangible 'place' where you go to surf - the ethereal world of computers and telecommunications on the internet.

data – Pieces of information (singular: datum). Data can exist in many forms such as numbers in a spreadsheet, text in a document, or as binary numbers stored in a computer's memory.

database – A store of information in digital form. Many web sites make use of substantial databases to deliver maximum content at high speed to the web user.

delete – You may want to delete old or unwanted files from a computer. Pressing the delete button may appear to delete the file, but in reality it only deletes the visible reference to the file. The data itself and any backup copies will usually remain on the hard drive, easily retrievable with software tools until permanently overwritten.

dial up account – This allows you to connect your computer to your internet provider's computer remotely.

digital – Based on the two binary digits, 1 and 0. The operation of all computers is

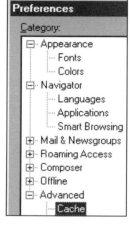

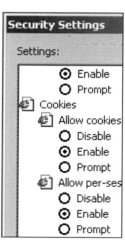

based on this amazingly simple concept. All forms of information are capable of being digitalised – numbers, words, and even sounds and images - and then transmitted over the internet.

digital signature – A unique personal signature specially created for use over the internet, designed to fulfil a similar function to the traditional handwritten signature used in ordinary life.

directory – On a personal computer (PC), a folder used to contain files.

DNS – Domain name server.

domain name – A name that identifies an IP address. It identifies to the computers on the rest of the internet where to access particular information. Each domain has a name. For someone@somewhere.co.uk, 'somewhere' is the domain name.

DOS – The disk operating system of a computer, such as MS DOS (Microsoft DOS).

download – To copy a file from one computer on the internet and save it onto your own computer.

ebusiness The broad concept of doing business to business, and business to consumer sales, over the internet.

ecommerce – The various means and techniques of transacting business online.

Echelon – The name of a governmental surveillance facility based in North Yorkshire, UK. Operated by the US, UK and certain other governments, it is said to be eavesdropping internet traffic using electronic dictionaries to trawl for key words in emails and other transmissions. See also **privacy**.

email – Electronic mail, any message or file you send from your computer to another computer using your 'email client' program (such as Netscape Messenger or Microsoft Outlook).

email address – The unique address given to you by your ISP. It can be used by others using the internet to send email messages to you. An example of a standard email address is: mybusiness@aol.com

emoticons – Popular symbols used to express emotions in email, for example the well known smiley :-) which means 'I'm smiling!' Emoticons are not normally appropriate for business communications.

encryption – The scrambling of information to make it unreadable without a key or password. Email and any other data can now be encrypted using PGP and other freely available programs.

ezines – The term for magazines and newsletters published on the internet.

FAQs – Frequently asked questions. You will see 'FAQ' everywhere you go on the internet. If you are ever doubtful about anything check the FAQ page, if the site has one, and you should find the answers to your queries.

Favorites – The rather coy term for **bookmarks** used by Internet Explorer, and by America Online. Maintaining a list of Favourites makes returning to a site easier.

file – A file is any specific body of data such as a word processed document, a spreadsheet, a database file, a graphics or video file, sound file, or computer program. On a PC, a file has a filename, and filename extension showing what type of file it is.

filtering software – Software loaded onto a computer to prevent access by someone to unwelcome content on the internet.

firewall – A firewall is special security software designed to stop the flow of certain files into and out of a computer network, e.g. viruses or attacks by hackers. A firewall would be an important feature of any fully commercial web site.

flame – A more or less hostile or aggressive message posted in a newsgroup or to an individual newsgroup user.

Glossary of internet terms ....

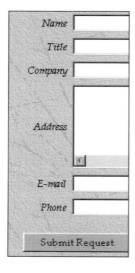

folder – The name for a directory on a computer. It is a place in which files are stored.

form – A web page that allows or requires you to enter information into fields on the page and send the information to a web site, program or individual on the web. Forms are often used for registration or sending questions and comments to web sites.

forums – Places for discussion on the internet. They include Usenet newsgroups, mailing lists, and bulletin board services.

frames – A web design feature in which web pages are divided into several areas or panels, each containing separate information. A typical set of frames in a page includes an index frame (with navigation links), a banner frame (for a heading), and a body frame (for text matter).

freespace – An allocation of free web space by an internet service provider or other organisation to its users or subscribers who want to publish their own web pages.

freeware – Software programs made available without charge. Where a small charge is requested, the term is **shareware**.

front page – The first page of your web site that the visitor will see. FrontPage is also the name of a popular web authoring package from Microsoft.

FTP – File transfer protocol the method the internet uses to speed files back and forth between computers. You don't need to worry about FTP unless you are thinking about creating and publishing your own web pages.

GIF – Graphic interchange format. It is a widely-used compressed file format used on web pages and elsewhere to display files that contain graphic images. See also **JPEG** and **PDF**.

Google – A well known and widely respected search engine: www.google.com

GUI – Graphic user interface. It describes the user-friendly screens found in Windows and other WIMP environments (Windows, icons, mice, pointers).

hacker – A person interested in computer programming, operating systems, the internet and computer security. The term can be used to describe a person who breaks into computer systems with the intention of pointing out the weaknesses in a system. In common usage, the term is often wrongly used to describe crackers.

header – The part of an email or newsgroup message which contains information about the sender and the route that the message took through the internet.

History list – A record of visited web pages. Your browser probably compiles a history list while you are surfing the web. It provides a handy way of revisiting web pages whose addresses you have forgotten to bookmark.

hits – The number of times the various components of a web page have been viewed.

home page This refers to the index page of an individual or an organisation on the internet. It usually contains links to related pages of information, and to other relevant sites

host – A host is the computer where a particular file or domain is located, and from where people can retrieve it.

HotBot – A popular internet search engine.

HTML – Hyper text markup language, the universal computer language used to create pages on the world wide web. It is much like word processing, but uses special 'tags' for formatting the text and creating hyperlinks to other web pages.

HTTP – Hypertext transfer protocol, the protocol used by the world wide web. It is the language spoken between your browser and the web servers. It is the standard way in which HTML documents are transferred from host computer to your local browser when you're surfing the internet. You'll see this acronym at the start of every web address, for example:

http://www.abcxyz.com

Nowadays, it is no longer necessary to enter 'http://' at the start of the address.

hyperlink – A hypertext phrase or image that calls up another web page when you click on it. Most web sites have lots of hyperlinks, or 'links' for short. These appear on the screen as buttons, images or bits of text (often underlined) that you can click on with your mouse to jump to another site on the world wide web.

hypertext – This is a link on an HTML page which, when clicked with a mouse, results in a further HTML page or graphic being loaded into view on your browser.

ICANN – The Internet Corporation for Assigned Names and Number, the body responsible for regulating domain names.

ICQ – A form of internet chat, derived from the phrase 'I seek you'. It enables users to be alerted whenever fellow users go online, so they can have instant chat communication. –

Infoseek – A popular internet search engine: www.infoseek.co.uk

Intel – Manufacturer of the Pentium, Celeron and other microprocessors for computers.

internet – The broad term for the fast-expanding network of global computers that can access each other in seconds by phone and satellite links. If you are using a modem on your computer, you too are part of the internet. The general term 'internet' encompasses email, web pages, internet chat, newsgroups, mailing lists, bulletin boards, and video conferencing. It is rather like the way we speak of 'the printed word' when we mean books, magazines, newspapers, newsletters, catalogues, leaflets, tickets and posters. The 'internet' does not exist in a single place any more than 'the printed word' does.

internet2 – A new form of the internet being developed exclusively for educational and academic use.

internet account – The account set up by your internet service provider which gives you access to the world wide web, electronic mail facilities, newsgroups and other value added services.

internet directory – A special web site which consists of information about other sites. The information is classified by subject area and further subdivided into smaller categories. The biggest and most widely used is Yahoo! at: www.yahoo.com. See also **search engines**.

Internet Explorer – The world's most popular browser software, a product of Microsoft and leading the field against Netscape (which is now owned by America Online).

internet keywords – A commercial service that allows people to find a domain name without having to type in www or .com

internet protocol (IP) number – The numerical code that is a domain's true address.

internet service providers – ISPs are commercial, educational or official organisations which offer people ('users') access to the internet. The well-known commercial ones in the UK include AOL, BT Internet, CompuServe, Demon, Freeserve, NTL and Virgin Net. Services typically include access to the world wide web, email and newsgroups, as well as others such as news, chat, and entertainment. Keep in mind that your internet service provider is in a position to see everything you do on the internet – emails sent and received, web sites visited, information downloaded, key words typed into search engines, newsgroups visited and messages read and posted. UK users should be aware of the new Regulation of Investigatory Powers Act (see RIP below).

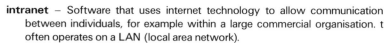

intranet – Software that uses internet technology to allow communication between individuals, for example within a large commercial organisation. t often operates on a LAN (local area network).

IP address – An 'internet protocol' address. All computers linked to the internet have one. The address is somewhat like a telephone number, and consists of four sets of numbers separated by dots.

IPv6 – A new internet coding system that will allow even more domain names.

IRC – Internet relay chat. Chat is an enormously popular part of the internet, and there are all kinds of public and private chat rooms and chat software. The chat involves typing messages which are sent and read in real time.

ISDN – Integrated services digital network. This is a high-speed telephone network that can send computer data from the internet to your PC faster than a normal telephone line.

Java – A programming language developed by Sun Microsystems to use the special properties of the internet to create graphics and multimedia applications on web sites.

JavaScript – A simple programming language that can be put onto a web page to create interactive effects such as buttons that change appearance when you position the mouse over them.

JPEG or **JPG** – The acronym is short for Joint Photographic Experts Group. A JPEG is a specialised file format used to display graphic files on the internet.

key shortcut – Two keys pressed at the same time. Usually the Control key (Ctrl), Alt key, or Shift key combined with a letter or number. For example, to use Control-D, press Control, tap the D key once firmly then take your finger off the Control key.

keywords – Words that sum up a web site for being indexed in search engines. For example for a cosmetic site the key words might include beauty, lipstick, make-up, fashion, cosmetic and so on.

LAN – A local area network, a computer network usually located in one building or campus.

link – See **hyperlink**.

Linux – A new widely and freely available operating system for personal computers.

LINX – The London Internet Exchange, the facility which maintains UK internet traffic in the UK.

log on/log off – To access/leave a network. In the early days of computing this literally involved writing a record in a log book. You may be asked to 'log on' to certain sites and particular pages. This normally means entering your user ID in the form of a name and a password.

macros – 'Macro languages' are used to automate repetitive tasks in Word processors and other applications.

mail server – A remote computer that enables you to send and receive emails. Your internet access provider will usually provide your mail server.

mailing list – A forum where messages are distributed by email to the members of the forum. A good place to find mailing lists is Liszt: www.liszt.com

marquee – A moving (scrolling) line of text on a web site, used for eye-catching purposes.

Media Player – Windows software on a personal computer that will play sounds and images including video clips and animations.

metasearch engine – A site that sends a keyword search to many different search engines and directories so you can use many search engines from one place.

meta tags – The keywords used in web page code to help search engine software rank the web site.

Microsoft – The world's biggest producer of software for personal computers, including the Windows operating systems, and the web browser Internet Explorer.

modem – This is an internal or external piece of hardware plugged into your PC. It links into a standard phone socket, thereby giving you access to the internet. The word derives from MOdulator and DEModulator.

MPEG or **MPG** – The file format used for video clips available on the internet. See also JPEG.

MP3 – An immensely popular audio format that allows you to download and play music on your computer. See: www.mp3.com

navigate – To click on the hyperlinks on a web site in order to move to other web pages or internet sites.

net – A slang term for the internet. In the same way, the world wide web is often just called the web.

netiquette – Popular term for the unofficial rules and language people follow to keep electronic communication in an acceptably polite form.

Netmeeting – A Microsoft plug-in that allows a moving video picture to be contained within a web page.

Netscape – After Microsoft's Internet Explorer, Netscape Navigator is the most popular browser for surfing the internet. The complete suite called Netscape Communicator includes the browser, plus Messenger (with email manager, a newsreader for newsgroups, and address book), plus a web page composer.

newsgroup – A newsgroup is a public collection of email-type messages on a particular topic. Messages can be placed within the newsgroup by anyone including you. The 80,000-plus newsgroups are collectively referred to as Usenet.

newsreader – A type of software that enables you to search, read, post and manage messages in a newsgroup. It will normally be supplied by your internet service provider when you first sign up, or preloaded on your new computer. The best known are Microsoft Outlook, and Netscape Messenger.

news server – A remote computer (e.g. your internet service provider) that enables you to access newsgroups.

nick – Nickname, an alias you can give yourself and use when entering a chat channel, rather than using your real name.

Notepad – The most basic type of word processor that comes with a Windows PC. To find it, click Start, Programs, then Accessories. Its more powerful cousin is Wordpad.

online – The time you spend linked via a modem to the internet. You can keep your phone bill down by reducing online time. The opposite term is offline.

OS – The operating system in a computer, for example MS DOS (Microsoft Disk Operating System), or Windows 95/98.

packet – The term for any small piece of data sent or received over the internet on your behalf by your internet service provider, and containing your address and the recipient's address. One email message for example may be transmitted as several different packets of information, reassembled at the other end to recreate the message.

password – A word or series of letters and numbers that enables a user to access a file, computer or program. A passphrase is a password made by using more than one word.

patch – A small piece of software used to patch up ('fix') a hole or defect ('bug') in a software program.

PC – Personal computer, based on IBM technology. It is distinct from the Apple Macintosh which uses a different operating system

PDA – Personal data assistant, a mobile phone, palm top or any other hand-held processor, typically used to access the internet.

PDF – Portable document format, a handy type of file produced using Adobe

Getting Started

My.MP3
MP3.com Mess
Store - Free Extr

Free Music

lome   Search   Guide

e: http://www.netscape.com

Chat   WebMail   My

N **Netsca**

Untitled - Notepad
File   Edit   Search   H

Notepad enables
plain, simple t
any formatting
complications.
want small file:
understood by v:
computer, which
want on the int

Passwords

PGP Security Products

▶ Overview
  Gauntlet Firewall
  CyberCop
  PGP VPN
  PGP Data Security
  PGP E-Business
  Server
  PGP Developer Kit
  PGP Freeware
  WebShield

Acrobat software. It has universal applications for text and graphics.

Pentium – The name of a very popular microprocessor chip in personal computers, manufactured by Intel.

PGP – Pretty Good Privacy. An extremely secure and freely available method of encoding a message before transmitting it over the internet.

ping – You can use a ping test to check the connection speed between your computer and another computer.

plug-in – A type of (usually free and downloadable) software required to add functionality to web page viewing. A good example is Macromedia Shockwave which enables you to view animations.

PoP – Point of presence. This refers to the dial-up phone numbers available from your ISP. All the major ISPs have local numbers covering the whole of the country.

portal site – Portal means gateway. It is any web site designed as a jumping off point from which you can explore all or part of the web.

privacy – Unless you take precautions, you have practically no personal privacy online. Almost all online activity can be electronically logged, analysed and archived by internet organisations, government agencies, police or other surveillance services. To explore internet privacy issues worldwide visit the authoritative Electronic Frontier Foundation web site at www.eff.org, and for the UK, www.netfreedom.org

program – A series of coded instructions designed to automatically control a computer in carrying out a specific task. Programs are written in special languages including Java, JavaScript, VBScript, and ActiveX.

protocol – An agreed method by which computers communicate over the internet. For example, for viewing web pages your computer would use hypertext transfer protocol (http). For downloading and uploading files, it would use file transfer protocol (ftp). It's not something to worry too much about in ordinary life.

proxy – An intermediate computer or server, used for reasons of security.

Quicktime – A popular free software program from Apple Computers. It is designed to play sounds and images including video clips and animations on both Apple Macs and personal computers.

radio button – A button that, when you click it, looks like this: ⦿

refresh, reload – The refresh or reload button on your browser toolbar tells the web page you are looking at to reload.

register – You may have to give your name, personal details and financial information to some sites before you can continue to use the pages.

RIP – The Regulation of Investigatory Powers Act (UK), a recent (2000) piece of legislation which gives the British police new powers of surveillance of people's use of the internet, for example by linking them into the major internet service providers using so-called 'black boxes'.

router – A machine that direct internet data (network packets) from one internet location to another.

rules – The term for message filters in Outlook Express.

scroll, scroll bar – To scroll means to move part of a page or document into view or out of view on the screen. Scrolling is done by using a scroll bar activated by the mouse pointer. Grey scroll bars automatically appear on the right and/or lower edge of the screen if the page contents are too big to fit into view.

search engine – A web site you can use for finding something on the internet. Popular search engines have developed into big web sites and information centres in their own right. There are hundreds of them. Among the best known are AltaVista, Google, Infoseek, Lycos, Metasearch and Webcrawler.

secure servers – The hardware and software provided so that people can use their credit cards and leave other details without the risk of others seeing them online. Your browser will tell you when you are entering a secure site.

server – Any computer on a network that serves information to other computers. Examples on the internet include web servers, mail servers and news servers.

shareware – Software that you can try before you buy.

Shockwave – A popular piece of software (or 'plug-in') produced by Macromedia, which enables you to view animations and other special effects on web sites. You can download it free and in a few minutes from Macromedia's web site. The effects can be fun, but they slow down the speed at which the pages load into your browser window.

signature file – This is a little text file in which you can place your address details, for adding to email and newsgroup messages.

smiley – A form of **emoticon**.

snail mail – The popular term for the standard postal service involving post-persons, vans, trains, planes, sacks and sorting offices.

spam– The popular term for electronic junk mail – unsolicited and unwelcome email messages sent across the internet.

SSL – Secure socket layer, a key part of internet security technology.

subscribe – The term for accessing a newsgroup or internet mailing list.

surfing – Slang term for browsing the internet, especially following trails of links on pages across the world wide web.

TCP/IP – Transmission control protocol/internet protocol, the essential technology of the internet. It's not normally something to worry about.

telnet – Software that allows you to connect via the internet to a remote computer and work as if you were a terminal linked to that system.

thumbnail – A small version of a graphic file which, when clicked, displays a larger version.

top level domain – The last code in the domain name of a web site, such as .com or .uk

traffic – The amount of data flowing across the internet, to a particular web site, newsgroup or chat room, or as emails.

trojan horse – A program that seems to perform a useful task but is really a malevolent program designed to cause damage to a computer system. See also virus.

UNIX – A computer operating system that has been in use for many years, and still is used in many larger systems. Most ISPs use it.

uploading – The act of copying files from your PC to a server or other PC on the internet, for example when you are publishing your own web pages. The term is most commonly used to describe the act of copying HTML pages onto the internet via FTP.

URL – Uniform resource locator, the address of each internet page. For instance the full URL of Internet Handbooks is:

http://www.internet-handbooks.co.uk

Usenet – The collection of more than 80,000 newsgroups that make up a substantial part of the internet.

virtual reality – The presentation of a lifelike scenario in electronic form. It can be used for gaming, business or educational purposes.

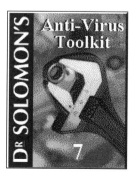

virus – A computer program maliciously designed to cause havoc to people's computer files. Viruses can typically be received when downloading program files from the internet, or from copying material from infected disks. Even Word files can be infected. Using anti-virus software is strongly recommended. See also trojan horse.

WAP – Wireless application protocol, new technology that enables mobile phones to access the internet.

web – Short for the world wide web. See **WWW** below.

Glossary of internet terms  . . . .

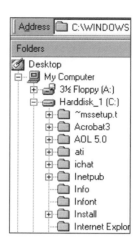

web client – Another term for a web browser.

webmaster – Any person who manages a web site.

web page – A web page is a file, with the filename extension .htm or .html, designed to be viewed on the world wide web. A typical web page includes a unique URL (address), headings, text, images, and hyperlinks (usually in the form of graphic icons, or underlined text). One web page usually contains links to lots of other web pages, either within the same web site or elsewhere on the world wide web.

web ring – A network of interlinked web sites that share a common interest.

web site – A set of web pages, owned or managed by the same person or organisation, and which are interconnected by hyperlinks.

Windows – The ubiquitous operating system for personal computers developed by Bill Gates and the Microsoft Corporation. The Windows 3.1 version was followed by Windows 95, Windows 98 and Windows 2000.

wizard – A feature of many software programs that guides you through its main stages, for example with the use of readymade templates.

WWW – The world wide web. Since it began in 1994 this has become the most popular part of the internet. The web is now made up of more than a billion web pages of every imaginable description, typically linking to other pages.

WYSIWYG – 'What you see is what you get.' If you see it on the screen, then it should look just the same when you print it out.

Yahoo! – The world's most popular internet directory and search engine: www.yahoo.com

Index

Index ....

Building a Web Site on the Internet
A practical guide to writing and commissioning web pages
Brendan Murphy BSc(Hons)

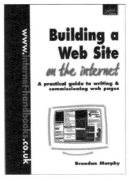

This book meets the urgent need for all business users who need an effective internet presence. Written in plain English, it explains the three main ways of achieving this: create it yourself by writing HTML, create it yourself by using a popular software package, or create it by hiring a web development company. Whether your organisation is large or small, make sure *you* make the right choices for your web site. Brendan Murphy BSc MBA MBSC teaches HNC in Computing, and lectures on the internet for the Open University. He is a Member of the British Computer Society, and Institute of Management Information Systems.
1 84025 314 2

Careers Guidance on the Internet
An essential guide to careers and vocational guidance resources online
Laurel Alexander

Are you planning to apply for a new job, or seeking promotion, or looking for new skills? Perhaps you are responsible for providing careers guidance to adults or young people? Careers information – like so many other things – is being challenged and revolutionised by the internet. New internet knowledge and skills are urgently needed by every professional working in this vital field. Packed with expert advice, and concise reviews of key web sites, this timely book will help you take full advantage of some amazing new online resources. Laurel Alexander MIPD MICG is a qualified trainer, assessor and guidance specialist.
1 84025 351 7

Discussion Forums on the Internet
A practical step-by-step guide to newsgroups, mailing lists and bulletin board services
Kye Valongo

A vast number of messages are posted into newsgroups, mailing lists and bulletin board services every day, and millions of people all over the world love to read them. These forums cover every imaginable subject, from local interest to jobs and travel, education, finance, entertainment, raunchy sex and scandal, culture and politics, computing and more. But how do you access them? Are they censored? How do you read the messages, and post messages yourself? Written in plain English, this guide tells you everything you need to know to explore this lively and ever controversial side of the internet. Kye Valongo is a qualified teacher, computer analyst, internet journalist and former Education Officer for IBM.
1 84025 329 0

Education & Training on the Internet
An essential resource for students, teachers, and education providers
Laurel Alexander MIPD MICG

Confused by search engines? Fed up with floods of irrelevant information? This is a much-needed new guide to today's exploding new world of education and training online. It includes reviews of top web sites of every imaginable kind – for education and training providers, schools, colleges, universities, training centres, professional organisations, resource suppliers, individuals, business organisations and academic institutions. Whether you are planning to study online, or are planning the delivery of online education and training, you will find this a key resource. Laurel Alexander MIPD MICG is a qualified trainer, assessor and guidance specialist.
1 84025 346 0

Other Internet Handbooks ....

Finding a Job on the Internet
Amazing new possibilities for jobseekers everywhere
Brendan Murphy BSc (Hons) MBA MBSC

Thinking of looking for a new job, or even a change of career? The internet is a great place to start your job search. In easy steps and plain English, this new guide explains how to find and use internet web sites and newsgroups to give you what you need. School, college and university leavers will find it invaluable for identifying suitable employers and getting expert help with CVs and job applications. The book will also be useful for career advisers and employers thinking of using the internet for recruitment purposes. Brendan Murphy BSc MBA MBSC teaches HNC in Computing, and lectures for the Open University.
1 84025 3657 – 2nd edition

Getting Connected to the Internet
A practical step-by-step guide for everyone
Ian Hosker

This book is intended for every PC owner who has not yet connected to the internet, but wants to do so provided they can feel confident about the process. It addresses all the questions commonly asked by the first-time subscriber. For example, what's the benefit of being online? What is an internet service provider (ISP)? What equipment do I need? What do I have to do, step-by-step? How do I send my first email? The book guides you carefully through all the initial stages. It shows how to get your computer ready, and how to load the required software from a CD. It explains how to create multiple email accounts, and perhaps most important of all, what to do if things don't go quite according to plan. Ian Hosker BEd(Hons) MSc is CVET Coordinator at the College of SS Mark & John in Plymouth.
1 84025 374 6

Getting Started on the Internet
A practical step-by-step guide for beginners
Kye Valongo

In plain English, this steps you through all the basics of the internet. It shows you how to obtain free access to the internet, how to set up your computer, how to look for information, and how to send and receive emails. It explains how to explore newsgroups and internet chat, how to protect your privacy online, and even how to create your own home page. Whether you want the internet for use at home, in education or in the workplace, this is the book for you, specially designed to get you up and running with the minimum fuss and bother. Kye Valongo is a qualified teacher, computer analyst, internet journalist and former Education Officer for IBM.
1 84025 321 5

Internet Explorer on the Internet
A step-by-step guide to using your browser
Kye Valongo

This book tells you all about Internet Explorer, the world's most popular and powerful browser. In practical steps, it explains how to use it for surfing the internet, how to send and read email messages using Outlook, and how to manage your electronic Address Book. Learn how to store selected web pages as Favourites (bookmarks). Discover how to disable irritating cookies. Find out how to control or delete sensitive computer files. If you are using Internet Explorer, or sharing access to a computer, this book will boost both your pleasure and protection when using the internet. Kye Valongo is a qualified teacher, computer analyst, internet journalist and former Education Officer for IBM.
1 84025 334 7

The Internet for Schools
A practical step-by-step guide for teachers, student teachers, parents and governors
Barry Thomas & Richard Williams

This title is aimed at teachers, student teachers, parents and school governors – in fact anyone interested in using the internet in primary and secondary education. The format is entertaining with key points highlighted. Each chapter is free-standing and should take no more than fifteen minutes to read. A major aim is to explain things in clear, non-technical and non-threatening language. There are detailed reviews of many key educational internet sites. Written by two experienced IT teachers, the book is UK focused, and contains typical examples and practical tasks that could be undertaken with students.
1 84025 302 9

The Internet for Students
Making the most of the new medium for study and fun
David Holland ACIB

Are you a student needing help with the internet to pursue your studies? Not sure where to start? – then this Internet Handbook is the one for you. It's up to date, full of useful ideas of places to visit on the internet, written in a clear and readable style, with plenty of illustrations and the minimum of jargon. It is the ideal introduction for all students who want to add interest to their studies, and make their finished work stand out, impressing lecturers and future employers alike. The internet is going to bring about enormous changes in modern life. As a student, make sure you are up to speed.
1 84025 306 1 – Reprinted

The Internet for Writers
Using the new medium to research, promote and publish your work
Nick Daws BSc (Hons)

This guide offers all writers with a complete introduction to the internet – how to master the basic skills, and how to use this amazing new medium to create, publish and promote your creative work. Would you like to broaden and speed up your research? Meet fellow writers, editors and publishers through web sites, newsgroups, or chat? Even publish your work on the internet for a potentially enormous new audience? Then this is the book you need, with all the practical starting points to get you going, step by step. The book is a selection of *The UK Good Book Guide.*
1 84025 308 8

Marketing Your Business on the Internet (2nd edition)
A practical step-by-step guide for all business owners and managers
Sara Edlington

Written by someone experienced in marketing on the internet from its earliest days, this practical book will show you step-by-step how to make a success of marketing your organisation on the internet. Discover how to find a profitable on-line niche, know which ten essential items to have on your web site, how to keep visitors returning again and again, how to secure valuable on- and off-line publicity for your organisation, and how to build your brand online. The internet is set to create phenomenal new marketing opportunities – make sure you are ready to win your share.
1 84025 364 9 (2nd edition)

Other Internet Handbooks....................................

Where to Find It on the Internet (2nd edition)
Your complete guide to search engines, portals, databases, yellow pages & other internet reference tools
Kye Valongo

Here is a valuable basic reference guide to hundreds of carefully selected web sites for everyone wanting to track down information on the internet. Don't waste time with fruitless searches – get to the sites you want, fast. This book provides a complete selection of the best search engines, online databases, directories, libraries, people finders, yellow pages, portals, and other powerful research tools. A recent selection of *The Good Book Guide*, and now in a new edition, this book will be an essential companion for all internet users, whether at home, in education, or in the workplace. Kye Valongo is a qualified teacher, computer analyst, internet journalist and former Education Officer for IBM.
1 84025 369 X – 2nd edition

Working from Home on the Internet
A practical illustrated guide for everyone
Laurel Alexander MIPD MICG

Would you like to work from home and earn good money using communications technology and the internet? More than 300 top sites are reviewed in this book which detail business opportunities on the internet, employers who use home workers and teleworkers, as well as recruitment agencies for IT and internet work. There are also sections on finding capital, legislation for the self employed, support for home workers (including disabled workers), business services and suppliers on the internet, and internet-based learning. Laurel Alexander MIPD MICG is a qualified trainer, assessor and guidance specialist.
1 84025 371 1

Your Privacy on the Internet
Everything you need to know about protecting your privacy and security online
Kye Valongo

Is Big Brother watching you? Many people will be shocked to hear that eavesdropping on private electronic communication is relatively easy and commonplace. This book explores the alarming way in which governments, companies and hackers are all using the internet to threaten your privacy. It also explains the various types of software you can use to prevent snooping and protect your privacy, whether you are browsing web pages, sending or receiving emails, accessing newsgroups, using search engines, or transmitting or receiving any kind of data online. The new borderless world is changing the whole way we live. Stay alert, and keep ahead. Kye Valongo is a qualified teacher, computer analyst, internet journalist and former Education Officer for IBM.
1 84025 355 X

Promoting a Web Site on the Internet
A practical step-by-step guide for everyone
Graham Jones BSc (Hons)

Do you know how to get your web site listed by the main search engines? Should you pay people to promote your web site? What are banner ads and web rings? This book shows you step-by-step how to plan and carry out the promotion of a new web site. It explains how to use the main search engines and internet indexes, how to use commercial services to get your web site noticed, and how to track down and use various new kinds of cooperative online help. Why not use traditional promotion methods, too? Surprisingly few internet operators use media such as print, mail or radio to promote their web sites. Yet traditional methods reach a wider public and can bring your site to the attention of a huge audience. This book shows you how to maximise both new and traditional promotional techniques, to give your new site the best chance of success.
1 84025 354 1